William Faulkner
A Study in Humanism, from Metaphor to Discourse

William Faulkner

A Study in Humanism
From Metaphor to Discourse
By Joseph Gold

University of Oklahoma Press
Norman

66-9093

Library of Congress Catalog Card Number: 66-13428

Copyright 1966 by the University of Oklahoma Press, Publishing Division of the University. Composed and printed at Norman, Oklahoma, U.S.A., by the University of Oklahoma Press. First Edition.

To my parents and their people:
   They Endured

Preface

Interest in William Faulkner has of recent years produced a regular beehive of critical industry. My excuse for adding to the already enormous production must be partly that my interest and pleasure was aroused and sustained by the excellent work of others. To all those who have written about Faulkner, I am indeed grateful. The things one reads all leave their mark, whether the reader is aware of it or not, and I would be hard put to it to say from which critical works I have learned the most. The same is surely true of one's encounters with people. In both cases, however, there is one exception: It is easy for me to acknowledge my debt to Frederick Hoffman. In his writings, in his seminars, and in his conversation, he instructed me. It is no exaggeration to say that he taught me to read and to write, as he must have taught many others. I cannot repay my debt to him.

To the English Department in the University of Wisconsin, and to Miss Helen White in particular, my thanks are due for giving me the opportunity to study and teach in the United States, where I learned about Americans and their incomparable literature. I am likewise grateful to the University of Manitoba for financial assistance in the preparation of this book, assistance which served as moral support as well as physical. I see that acknowledgments have a way of stretching out beyond one's anticipation. I have not mentioned my typist nor her diligent work, my colleagues, my students, and my friends. I hope they will take credit for whatever merit is in this work. Without the patience of my wife, Sandra, there might have been no critic, let alone criticism. My debt to her is a genuine scholarly one, as well as personal. In either case, nothing I can write here will indicate the true extent of my gratitude.

I suppose that what follows is sufficient testimony to my adulation of William Faulkner himself. For those of us who see his work as a great testament to the dignity of man, his death was a stunning grief, the obliteration of light. His legacy, however, is inexhaustible. Our gratitude will be expressed by reading and teaching it as truthfully as we can.

JOSEPH GOLD

December, 1965
Winnipeg, Manitoba

Contents

William Faulkner
A Study in Humanism, from Metaphor to Discourse

In the higher poetry, an enlightened Critic chiefly looks for a reflection of the wisdom of the heart and the grandeur of the imagination. Wherever these appear, simplicity accompanies them; Magnificence herself when legitimate, depending upon a simplicity of her own, to regulate her ornaments.

. . . so that we shall find that no poetry has been more subject to distortion, than that species, the argument and scope of which is religious; and no lovers of the art have gone farther astray than the pious and the devout.

—WILLIAM WORDSWORTH

CHAPTER I

Introduction
"What I was talking about"

When William Faulkner was in Japan in 1955, he made one statement which seems to me to stand out among his many public utterances as singularly revealing: "[To] me the Old Testament is some of the finest, most robust and most amusing folklore I know. The New Testament is philosophy and ideas, and something of the quality of poetry."[1] What gives this comment special significance, coming as it does from this particular author, is that it unwittingly describes a transition that has taken place in Faulkner's own work, dividing it roughly into those novels and stories written before he received the Nobel Prize and those written after.

There is no doubt that Faulkner's description of the Old Testament is a convincing one. There is a power and a color, a vivid intensity in the characterization, a vitality in narration, a beauty in the language, a general dynamism that is incomparable. Dogma and theology are conveniently confined to the first five books, leaving the rest free for metaphor and narration with the grandeur of myth. Everything is concrete and alive and human, and only the vigorous drawings of a Blake could give the work an even remotely adequate pictorial rendering. The God of the Old Testament speaks, acts, and feels, and rapidly emerges with a strong personality comprehended as a force acting in and through the doings of men. On the other hand, the New Testament, as Faulkner pointed

[1] Robert A. Jelliffe (ed.), *Faulkner at Nagano* (Tokyo, 1956), 45; hereafter cited as *Nagano*.

3

out, is an intellectual extension and elaboration of the Old, an attempt to explain, to make rationally apprehensible the nature of God, man, and Heaven and to prescribe a pattern of conduct and attitude by which man can attain eternal life. The New Testament is a book of ideas; God, though He is a prominent part of the subject matter, stays essentially in the background. We may believe that He is there, but we never see Him, hear Him, or feel Him.

Now all this seems fairly obvious, and these observations would hardly be worth making, were it not for the fact that they are equally applicable to Faulkner's writing, falling as it does into two phases, two bodies of work, roughly divided by World War II. Indeed, perhaps it was that war, or perhaps it was international public recognition, finally symbolized and made real for Faulkner by the Nobel Prize, that caused this shift in his writing. Whatever the reason, there is a major stylistic shift, and it seems to be characterized by the same distinctions that separate the literary features of the Old and New Testaments. One detects in Faulkner's later fiction an urgency, almost a desperation, to convince and explain. There is an overabundance of rhetoric and speech-making, dragged into the novels with little justification; there is an emphasis on ideas rather than on people—altogether a concentration on saying rather than on doing. When the critic takes into account the religious tone of what Faulkner is saying (for instance in a work like *Requiem for a Nun*), there is a natural temptation to relate this later emphasis to the author's sudden realization that he was a figure of international prominence, called upon by his eminence to serve as a spokesman for mankind.

In his early work Faulkner approaches the creation of myth. That is to say, his characters are so convincing and universal and so recognizable that they attain the stature of archetypes

4

while retaining the complexities of human beings. Their actions evolve into metaphors about the nature of human experience. In contrast, after 1948, Faulkner created Christ-figures instead of Christ-like figures. Faulkner's language must reasonably be called unjustifiable rhetoric when it bears little relationship to its subject. The complexity of the language that is applied to Joe Christmas is appropriate because of the equally complex agony of the character's psyche and situation, but this kind of writing becomes mere verbal gymnastics when applied to a character as decided and single-minded and untroubled as the corporal in *A Fable*.

This major shift in emphasis can be illustrated by what happened in the composition of the last two works of the Snopes trilogy. *The Town* and *The Mansion* seem to have come from an artist who was torn between a compulsion to sermonize and a wish to recapture the vigor of the imaginative early work. The frequent use of early-story material in these novels would seem to illustrate this latter desire, while the persistent use of Gavin Stevens and his rhetorical tendencies indicates that Faulkner could not overcome his need to make forthright and unveiled statements.

The first real indication of this pulpit tendency is observable in the 1942 version of "The Bear," which heralds the coming of what might be called the public years. To that story, which had its origins years before, Faulkner added a long, sententious debate between Isaac and his cousin McCaslin which amounts to an analysis of the significance and meaning of what has passed before in the more convincing narrative part of the story. Faulkner is virtually being his own commentator, as though he feared that the ideas embodied in the action were not clear enough. If it be objected that the same technique was employed much earlier in *Absalom, Absalom!* we might observe that the Quentin-Shreve discussion differs substantially from the Ike-McCaslin debate by virtue of the difference in context. Quentin's opinion is merely one of a number of points of view on which the novel is constructed. His discussion with Shreve is not about the events of the novel—it is a method by which the events are actually revealed. The novel's fabric is tightly woven together, and from the beginning Quentin is shown to be striving desperately to understand the implications of the events that emerge in the telling. In other words, Quentin's reactions to events are not separated in time or space from the events themselves. Quentin is a convincing part of the problematical world of the South which he carries around with him. His exchanges with Shreve are woven into the complex relationships and intricate psychological explorations that characterize the fictional technique. None of these observations can be convincingly applied to Isaac of "The Bear," who is a different person in his debate with his cousin from the younger Ike of the earlier hunting episodes. He has shifted in time and place and thus "stepped out," as it were, to comment on his own actions.

What then is this "message" that Faulkner has felt driven to express, so overtly that it has altered the whole tone and shape of his work? Before we choose any one label for his position, let us look at some of the significant statements, public and fictional, that together constitute a consistent attitude towards man. The most obvious first choice is the Stockholm Address.

> [The writer] must teach himself that the basest of all things is to be afraid; and, teaching himself that, forget it forever, leaving no room in his workshop for anything but the old verities and truths of the heart, the old universal truths lacking which any story is ephemeral and doomed—love and honor and pity and pride and compassion and sacrifice. . . . I believe that man will not merely endure: he will prevail. He is immortal, not because

he alone among creatures has an inexhaustible voice, but because he has a soul, a spirit capable of compassion and sacrifice and endurance.[2]

In Japan, Faulkner made similar statements about the goals of writers like the following:

Q: I think that what you said just now is a very good and proper message for us, but if there is any other thing that you can say to encourage us . . . .

F: Yes—to work, to believe always in man, that man will prevail, that there's no suffering, no anguish, that man is not suitable to changing, if he wants to, then to work hard.[3]

F: People can always be saved from injustice by some man. . . . Anyone can save anyone from injustice if he just will, if he just tries, just raises his voice. . . .[4]

We must cure them [errors]; we mustn't go back to a condition, an idyllic condition, in which the dream [made us think] we were happy, we were free of trouble and sin. We must take the trouble and sin along with us, and we must cure that trouble and sin as we go.[5]

He's [the writer] not really writing about his environment, he's simply telling a story about human beings in the terms of environment . . . . The novelist is talking about people, about man in conflict with himself, his fellows, or his environment. . . .[6]

I still believe in man. That he still wishes, desires, wants to do better than he knows he can and occasionally he does do a little better than anybody expects of him. This man [is immortal]. . . .[7]

Well, I believe in God. Sometimes Christianity gets pretty debased, but I do believe in God, yes. I believe that man has a

[2] "The Stockholm Address," *American Literary Essays* (ed. by Lewis Leary) (New York, 1960), 313.
[3] *Nagano*, 18.
[4] *Ibid.*, 76.
[5] *Ibid.*, 77–78.
[6] *Ibid.*, 157.
[7] *Ibid.*, 5.

soul that aspires towards what we call God, what we mean by God. . . .[8]

I would say, and I hope, the only school I belong to, that I want to belong to, is the humanist school.[9]

I have quoted at length because the overwhelming impact of so many separate pronouncements cannot be ignored or treated lightly.

Consider again that at the University of Virginia, Faulkner said:

> Q: Sir, it means that your basic conception of life is optimistic?
> F: Yes.
> Q: But not of the individual.
> F: Well, the individual is not too much, he's only a pinch of dust, he won't be here very long anyway, but his species, his dreams, they go on. There's always somebody that will keep on creating the Bach and the Shakespeare as long as man keeps on producing. . . .[10]
>
> What we need are people who will say, This is bad and I'm going to do something about it, I'm going to change it.[11]
>
> . . . there is no place anymore where individual man can speak quietly to individual man of such simple things as honesty with oneself and responsibility towards others and protection for the weak and compassion and pity for all.[12]

The generally humanistic attitude that emerges so strongly seems, to judge from the fiction, to be grounded in a religious faith, a belief in God as a prevailing force of good when working through natural, instinctive, "innocent" man. *A Fable* is an allegory that retells the Christ myth in humanistic terms.

[8] *Ibid.*, 23–24.

[9] *Ibid.*, 95.

[10] Frederick L. Gwynn and Joseph L. Blotner (eds.), *Faulkner in the University* (Charlottesville, Virginia, 1959), 286.

[11] *Ibid.*, 246.

[12] *Ibid.*, 242.

It seems that for Faulkner, as for many Western writers and thinkers, Christ was a living instance of a man under the domination of the divine element in him. Like Emerson, Faulkner seems to believe in an immanent Christ. If Faulkner believes in God, it is in a God that resides in some way in the heart of man. Emerson says without the guise of fiction what Faulkner says in *A Fable*.

> Jesus Christ belonged to the true race of prophets. He saw with open eye the mystery of the soul. Drawn by its severe harmony, ravished with its beauty, he lived in it, and had his being there. Alone in all history he estimated the greatness of man. One man was true to what is in you and me. He saw that God incarnates himself in man, and evermore goes forth anew to take possession of his World. He said, in this jubilee of sublime emotion, "I am divine. Through me, God acts; through me, speaks. Would you see God, see me; or see thee, when thou also thinkest as I now think."[13]

God becomes man when man becomes God. Faulkner demonstrates this by having his old general, of *A Fable*, give man completely free choice in the matter of his own salvation.[14] God, in this later work, is not a controlling force but a kind of servant of human wishes. Man collectively controls his own destiny. Nancy, in *Requiem for a Nun*, is a drug addict, a whore, and finally a murderer, but she is "innocent," which is to say that she can never be condemned for wickedness of motivation because her intentions and the results of her acts, Faulkner would have us believe, are good. Faulkner is convinced, apparently, that no act can be good or evil in itself. He has plentifully peopled his novels to show that evil resides

[13] "The Divinity School Address," *Selections From Ralph Waldo Emerson* (New York, 1957), 105.

[14] A thorough discussion of the allegorical God of *A Fable* is contained in chapter six. See also *Modern Fiction Studies*, Vol. VII (Summer, 1961), 145–56.

in attitude. Grimm, Hines, Flem Snopes, Jason, Sutpen, Januarius Jones, and many others are people who commit acts which might also conceivably have been attributed to the "heroic" figures in the novels. What distinguishes them is their consciousness of their own separateness, their nonhuman estimates of others, and their insistence on the gratification of selfhood. They are cold and lack the compassion which is man's highest attribute.

The best illustration of this attitude is in Faulkner's treatment of man's relationship to nature. Old Ben, the bear, is the incarnation of innocence; he is incapable of evil, killing as he does out of pure need or pure anger, but incapable of violating his natural integrity. "It [the bear] did things that were evil, by a more intelligent code, but by its own code they were not evil and it was strong and brave to live up to its own code of morality."[15] Thus he ought to be killed by an equally pure and appropriate force—killed, but killed with regret since compassion is the "code of morality" to which man must "live up." Isaac, for instance, shows equal respect for bear, deer, and snakes; the hunters in this story and the convict in the Old Man are able to live in perfect harmony with nature.[16] This concept is like nothing so much as William Blake's concept of innocence. It is a belief which involves the necessity and possibility of throwing over the past, of being better than one is, of creating paradise here and now in a world that is Eden if only we will see it and love it and in which man is either the creative or the destructive force depending on the choice he makes.

. . . He had created them, upon this land this South for which He had done so much with woods for game and streams for fish

15 *Nagano*, 93.

16 It is significant, however, that it is not Isaac who kills the bear. This situation is dealt with at length in chapter three.

10

and deep rich soil for seed and lush springs to sprout it and long summers to mature it and serene falls to harvest it and short mild winters for men and animals and saw no hope anywhere and looked beyond it where hope should have been.[17]

But Faulkner, unlike Blake, does not have his own carefully wrought mythology or a system of dialectic in which some part of man, like the imagination which Blake employs, can be considered the shaping and creative best impulse. Like "Humanism" itself, or any other strongly held religious conviction, Faulkner's belief is based on faith. Faulkner is therefore obliged to fall back on tradition and finds himself in the difficult position of selecting and reworking elements in a past to which he does not subscribe. He is unable to provide a "how" and can only show us an "is." This he does dynamically in his early work in the figures of people like Dilsey, Lena Grove, the tall convict, Nancy Mannigoe, Chick Mallison, Byron Bunch, and in the later work he does it by the more wooden presentation of characters like the corporal of *A Fable* and the Ratliff of his last two novels.

The nearest formal arrangement of these views that one can detect as an influence on Faulkner is the Baptist, revivalist, evangelistic tradition in the South, with which he must surely have come into contact and which he brilliantly depicts in the Negro church meeting in *The Sound and the Fury:*

> Remember, the writer must write out of his background. He must write out of what he knows and the Christian legend is part of any Christian's background, especially the background of a country boy, a Southern country boy. My life was passed, my childhood, in a very small Mississippi town, and that was a part of my background. I grew up with that. I assimilated that, took that in without even knowing it. It's just there.[18]

[17] William Faulkner, *Go Down, Moses* (New York, 1942), 283.

[18] Gwynn and Blotner (eds.), *Faulkner in the University*, 86.

The kind of religionism that Faulkner most likely encountered, permeating the South, is sought for through exhortation. It is a demand to vision through decision. "Believe," says Nancy Mannigoe, and the religious life is thus made to seem deceptively easy. Faulkner's heroes are most frequently simple-minded, sometimes country people, sometimes children, even idiots. They are chosen because in such people the wished-for state of mind is more readily observable. It is not their usual poverty or their often unfortunate physical situation that is offered to us for imitation, but the state of mind which they demonstrate by their living. When, as in his later fiction, Faulkner tries to intellectualize these beliefs, he fails on all fronts. He finds himself unable to systematize the faith which he advocates, and the effort required by the attempt undermines the imaginative conception which so powerfully infuses the fully realized and vividly delineated characters of the early novels. Had Faulkner tried carefully to explain why Dilsey is as she is, he would have been unable to visualize fully the completed person, and we would have received an early version of the pseudo-Christ of *A Fable*. Dilsey's very dynamism comes from a total, unexplained commitment. Like all of Faulkner's heroes, she is fully alive in the spirit and has no concern with doctrines and dogma and the intellectual minutiae of the religious word. Her faith represents the solid foundation of religion and signifies a distillation of the Christian idea. She is full of love and tolerance and, much of the time, even joy. This last characteristic is best illustrated, however, in Lena Grove, who moves through a hostile world transforming it by her trusting serenity into a place of mystery and wonder. She does not doubt that people are essentially good and kind, and in a magical way this assurance calls forth goodness and kindness.

Faulkner is unable to systematize in any way the absolutes towards which he seems to be imaginatively driven. However, we can glean a fairly consistent view which, though it is without the sanction of theology and though it lacks an explicable dialectic, does provide a forceful vision of the wished-for state of mind. Lena Grove and Dilsey most obviously represent the kind of attitude which not only makes their own lives possible and meaningful but also affects the world around them. In Christian evangelism there is a phrase about making "the decision for God." These noble women seem to have made this decision. They illustrate what happens when by an act of will one decides to believe in fundamental human goodness, in the possibility of human improvement, and in the essential oneness of man.

In at least three obvious cases Faulkner's heroic protagonists are women, which seems to indicate his perhaps romantic mistrust of reason and intellect as a means of attaining truth. Chick Mallison in *The Town* observes:

> Since women learn at about two or three years old and then forget it, the knowledge about their-selves that a man stumbles on by accident forty odd years later with the same kind of startled amazement of finding a twenty-five-cent piece in a old pair of britches you had started to throw away.[19]

And in *Go Down, Moses* Isaac thinks: *"They are born already bored with what a boy approaches only at fourteen and fifteen with blundering and aghast trembling."*[20] As women understand their own sexual natures, so they seem to understand their own relationship to the world, and so presumably, through feeling and emotion, one can arrive at a sense of

[19] William Faulkner, *The Town* (New York, 1957), 101.
[20] *Go Down, Moses*, 314.

mystery and wonder and unity in the universal situation in the way that Lena does. Such an ideal state has all the aspects of humanism, and leads to all the acts that Dilsey performs and that are embodied in other humanistic or existential twentieth-century works, for instance via the doctor of Camus' *La Peste*. But Faulkner's humanism rests on a rock foundation of faith, almost of mysticism. There is a God, and He is visible in the universe through man, and in nature. He is available to all men at all times if they will throw over systems and act out of acceptance and love. Faulkner can no more than any other "believer" transmit the means of spiritual commitment; he can only illustrate the appearance and the effect of such commitment.

Faulkner says that it is the writer's task to illustrate and elaborate the human qualities of "love and honor and pity and pride and compassion and sacrifice." By reoffering these "old verities," the artist reminds man of the best in himself and helps him to see the beauty, the nobility that is possible in life. And these qualities are not arrived at rationally; they are the "truths of the heart." One thinks of Wordsworth or the transcendentalists more than anyone else. By 1950 then, Faulkner clearly saw his role as that of a kind of preacher, an inspired illustrator and celebrant of man's basic qualities. But, as I have said above, this was not a new self-awareness that he came to. A glance at some of the early works, those written in the late 1920's and early 1930's, will, I hope, further reveal that Faulkner was always writing from a single point of view.

The "shift" then in Faulkner's writing is a shift of emphasis or technique, rather than a change of ideas, and it is perhaps illuminated by regarding it as a move from the making of myth to the construction of allegory. Perhaps it is necessary at this point to say something about literary symbolism. Language and therefore literature is structured on the use of symbols. The degree to which a reader's responses to symbols vary is the degree to which the symbols vary. For instance, a letter of the alphabet is not a symbol (except as it may be read aloud when it symbolizes a sound), but as a mark on paper it is a thing in itself. As part of a word it becomes an integral part of a symbol, as in "whale," where the word is designed to evoke a picture of a sea creature, already previsioned in the reader's mind. This is the simplest kind of symbol usage. The phrase "ferocious whale" enriches the mental picture by increasing the vitality of our necessary imaginative response. We move in our minds from a dictionary illustration, from a "still," to a "film strip." The phrase "white whale" enriches our response infinitely more (if we have read *Moby Dick*, though to some extent even if we have not), conjuring up the entire complex of ideas and images that constitute Melville's novel and all the emotional responses that he explains in the chapter on the "whiteness of the whale." We thus see that a literary symbolic structure is possible on three levels. A word produces an object; a phrase produces a qualified object; a series of phrases, an elaborate pattern, produces an object so qualified and of such complex associations that it in turn evokes something further, perhaps a whole range of associations. It may thus be said that symbols have a range of reference, some extending further in their association than others, as the ripples of water extend in proportion to the size of the disturbance.

I would say then that one way of distinguishing symbols is according to the degree of complexity of the emotional and intellectual response that they evoke in the reader. Now the nature of a symbol which represents an abstraction, as the white whale represents, say evil, is that it evokes a relatively great complexity of responses, or one might say, disturbances in the reader. This is so because no single image can be supplied to match the symbol, and the mind searches for equivalents and involuntarily produces associations in order to try to comprehend the abstract idea. In other words, such a symbol forces upon the intelligent reader the problem of encountering the concept for which it stands, and this is a stimulating exercise. I call this literary process, for want of a better term, associative symbolism, and, in specific instances, echoing symbols.

There is another kind of symbolism, which might be called directive, which works against richness and complexity in the literature where it is employed. This is because it uses symbolic equivalents or signs to call forth concrete secondaries. Such symbolism produces what Northrop Frye calls "naïve allegory" of the kind employed in local pageants and in some literature.[21] Echoing symbols, on the other hand, tend to produce myth and archetype.

In naïve allegory the object of the game is to find the shoe which fits the foot, and this is usually easy to do—must be easy to do since the writer is really only interested in secondaries, not in symbols, and therefore the literary construction is based on the assumption that the reader is a reasonably good judge of shoes and the author is an expert salesman. Once the reader has found the exact shoe, he has found it, and he is left with it. The scheme is simple because in such cases the author's motive is usually discursive rather than exploratory and his impulse is didactic rather than visionary. It may thus be seen that a collection of echoing symbols will increase the complexity and profundity of a work of art by a complex kind of progressive presentation, as three dimensions in chess would make the game more than 50 per cent more difficult. A collection of directive symbols, on the other hand, will produce no more

[21] *Anatomy of Criticism* (Princeton, N.J., 1957).

16

than what amounts to a repetition and duplication of a single symbol, as though one were to play the same game of chess again and again with different-colored pieces.

So far we have been cursorily discussing the over-all impact of kinds of symbolic fiction, what we might call the general dynamics of fiction. We must ask further how and why an echoing symbol differs in itself from a directive symbol. An echoing symbol is usually complex in itself and realistic. Thus, *Moby Dick* is interesting in his own right; he has a personality, a vitality, and a thorough characterization of his own. So, indeed, does Dilsey of *The Sound and the Fury*, Christian Pilgrim of *Pilgrim's Progress*, and Gulliver, along with countless other symbolic figures in the greatest literature. The corporal of *A Fable* does not have such characteristics—he is not real, not imaginable in human terms, and not an emotionally evocative figure, whereas his counterpart in *Light in August*, Joe Christmas, does have all the literary qualities that the former lacks. This situation is also true of the cardboard Nancy Mannigoe as opposed to the flesh-and-blood Dilsey, and, to a lesser extent, of Gavin Stevens, as he reappears from *Light in August* to *The Mansion*. In other words, Faulkner has moved from the presentation of archetypal images to the presentation of "disguised ideas." But why is a directive symbol, like the corporal, so different from Joe Christmas? Because the corporal is transposable for Christ and, in fact, Faulkner is primarily interested in Christ; the corporal is only an intellectual contrivance, not a product of the imagination. Joe Christmas, on the other hand, is not transposable for anything, and while he symbolizes many ideas and situations, he is still himself, the focus of a web of associations. In other words a symbolic figure of this kind is a total substitution for the ideas which we can thereafter abstract; being a synthesis, an integration, he is a new reality and not any one of the parts that compose him.

An allegorical symbol like the corporal is not a substitution, but a preparation for his equivalent. Concretions are not abstractions, the "Mona Lisa" is not enigma itself, so a concretion like Joe Christmas must absorb and embody the abstractions he represents and thus become all important in himself. Any critical analysis of such a figure must violate the completeness of the original literary construct, unless the critic ultimately returns to the whole man as he acts out his drama. The corporal, however, is not the corporal but somebody else and will, therefore, never be himself.

Now it seems that the degree of integrity produced by symbols results not from what the symbols represent, but from the motivation of the writer, as Mr. Frye points out.[22] In discursive writing, the power of the images is diminished while in truly literary constructs the precision or rigidity of the ideas is diminished.

When Faulkner answered a question at Virginia in the following way, he perhaps revealed more of himself than he knew:

> Q: Mr. Faulkner, in your speech at Stockholm you expressed great faith in mankind . . . not only to endure but to prevail . . . . Do you think that's the impression the average reader would get after reading *The Sound and the Fury?*
> F: . . . yes, that is what I was talking about in all the books, and I failed to say it.[23]

The increasing desire to speak about his faith in mankind led Faulkner to take a more conscious and a more desperate hand in planting that "talking" in his later work. Faulkner also said, "I wrote for years before it occurred to me that strangers might read the stuff, and I've never broken that habit."[24]

[22] *Ibid.*, 75.
[23] Gwynn and Blotner (eds.), *Faulkner in the University*, 4.
[24] *Ibid.*, 14.

But the latter part of the comment cannot be true—was not true because the Nobel Prize must have made Faulkner intensely aware all of the time that strangers were reading his "stuff." This awareness, coupled with his convictions, produced the state of affairs that is the subject of this approach. Faulkner described his own magnificient early work in fitting terms:

> You write a story to tell about people, man in his constant struggle with his own heart, with the hearts of others, or with his environment. It's man in the ageless, eternal struggles which we inherit and we go through as though they'd never happened before, shown for a moment in a dramatic instant of the furious motion of being alive, that's all my story is. You catch this fluidity which is human life and you focus a light on it and you stop it long enough for people to be able to see it.[25]

In his later writing, however, the people are not alive. Of "The Bear," Faulkner could say, "That is symbolism," but of the symbolism that critics have found in *The Sound and the Fury*, he said instead:

> Well, I would say that the author didn't deliberately intend but I think that in the same culture the background of the critic and of the writer are so similar that a part of each one's history is the seed which can be translated into the symbols which are standardized within that culture. That is, the writer don't have to know Freud to have written things which anyone who does know Freud can divine and reduce into symbols.[26]

Faulkner's personal history in the use of symbolism was clearly summarized in one other speech in Japan:

> And when I found that people read the books and got pleasure from them and found in them something of what I tried to put

25 *Ibid.*, 25.
26 *Ibid.*, 147.

[in], I was very pleased, I was very flattered. Though they found things in those books that I was too busy to realize I was putting in the books. They found symbolism that I had no background in symbolism to put in the books. But what symbolism is in the books is evidently instinct in man, not in man's knowledge but in his inheritance of his old dreams, in his blood, perhaps his bones, rather than in the storehouse of his memory, his intellect.[27]

Having been "pleased" and "flattered," Faulkner became self-conscious. He began to write of the old verities as his intellect now conceived them, and perhaps he started "putting in" a little symbolism, just to make sure that some was there.

[27] *Nagano*, 68.

CHAPTER II

Early Works
"The furious motion of being alive"

Although in his more recent fiction Faulkner has expressed himself with more vigor, his moral outlook and his philosophical views are to be found as the core of meaning in all his novels and many of the short stories. Mary Cooper Robb has summed up the growing refutation of that school of criticism which considered Faulkner to be a writer who, in his early work, was wallowing in horror and morbidity in order merely to shock his audience:

> His primary concern, after all, is to show that a man must choose between right and wrong, for one set of human values and against another. The choosing must inevitably involve conflict, which indeed, is one of the necessary ingredients of any story. But if we can differentiate among the various qualities which together make up "good," then "evil" may be departmentalized. To tell a story of courage the writer must also make clear the possibility of abject fear. If he writes of honor, he must also write of dishonor. Hope suggests a possible despair; pride, vanity; compassion, inhumanity; pity, mercilessness; and sacrifice, base selfpreservation. Failing to show or to make implicit these opposites the writer also fails to impart to his readers the intensity of experience they are seeking.[1]

Although the earlier writing differs in style and form from the later, the same themes are used to produce Faulkner's thesis about the human situation. To recapitulate these

[1] *William Faulkner: An Estimate of His Contribution to the American Novel* (Pittsburgh, 1957), 24.

themes: the past is a continual factor in shaping the present and is frequently an undesirable influence, since it hands down ready-made values as well as institutions; as a direct result of man's inevitable dependence on the past, the individual owes himself and the race the responsibility of examining and selecting from the values, traditions, and beliefs of the past. The "easy" answer is to refrain from examining, considering, and evaluating and to accept without question the values and beliefs that were and are current. There is no satisfaction, however, in an easy answer—as those, like Gerald Levine in *A Fable*, find out; the "easy" exits lead to dead ends. Satisfaction may be obtained only by facing reality and meeting with courage the problems that arise from awareness.

I do not wish, nor does space allow me in this study, to dwell on the early fiction. The major works of the 1930's have received abundant attention already. However, it seems essential to glance at the themes of the very early work in order that my subsequent comments will have some basis of reference. If Faulkner's outlook has not changed, we should know from what it has not changed. If his method of presenting major themes alters or changes its emphasis, we should see what it once was. The best way to do this, perhaps, is to glance at the characteristic themes and techniques of some of the major novels that constitute the heights of Faulkner's early achievement and also to consider the themes of some early and rarely examined stories and slighter novels to see how widely these themes were expressed. A criticism of weaknesses in the more recent fiction does not mean conversely that the early fiction was always flawless. It does seem, however, that the particular faults of Faulkner's later rhetoric were missing from his earlier work, even when that work failed in other ways. In any case, my general purpose is not to pass value judgments on Faulkner's writing but to indicate why the special failings of

the later writing have occurred and to attempt to show how they reveal a developing conscience that was always present.[2]

"That Will Be Fine," a story which first appeared in 1935, not only illustrates perfectly Faulkner's attitude towards past and present, but deals with a family that bears distinct resemblances to the Compsons. The story is told from the child's point of view. From the beginning, we see that the child is obsessed by money—all his thinking is geared to the acquisition of money, but unlike the "normal" child, he has no purpose in mind behind his greed. He desires money for its own sake, and he is willing, like a speculator, to spend a little to make more. The events take place at Christmas, which for this child is a good time for obtaining money. "Jesus, I can't hardly wait," he says.[3] The concept of "suffer little children" is thus ironically trampled underfoot by Faulkner's characters, for we soon see that instead of aspiring to the innocence of children, the adults in the story are directly responsible for the material values that are at the heart of this child's world. Whereas money is central to the world of the men, the women of the family are concerned, like Mrs. Compson in *The Sound and the Fury*, with meaningless and unrealistic clichés about family honor and name. The child has an uncle who lives by cheating, forgery, and adultery and by trading on the false "honor" myths of his sisters. He has, moreover, involved his nephew in his roguery, as an accomplice in his illicit assignations, on the promise of money-bribes which are never paid. The child is well trained in duplicity. This is the only training he receives, since pathetically his mother tries to keep him from reality: "And how Mr. Pruitt showed her with her own

---

[2] I have omitted mention of *The Hamlet* in the following glance at early work. Those interested in a similar study of this novel may see my article, "The 'Normality' of Snopesism: Universal Themes in Faulkner's *The Hamlet*," *Wisconsin Studies*, Vol. III (Winter, 1962), 25–34.

[3] *Collected Stories of William Faulkner* (New York, 1950), 266.

eyes the check with Grandpa's name signed to it and how even Aunt Louisa could see that Grandpa's name had been—and then Mamma said Louisa! Remember Georgie! and that was me."[4] Expecting a reward, the boy helps his uncle to a meeting with a married woman which leads to the uncle's death at the hands of the husband. The story clearly demonstrates that each generation is responsible for the values of the next. The uncle dies without paying his debt either literally or metaphorically to the boy, leaving him with only a heritage of deception. No one in fact does "Remember Georgie."

"A Rose for Emily" appeared in 1930. Emily, a figure from the past, grows to middle age without marrying. She is a symbol of the past as well as a fully realized pathetic figure. When all hope for marriage seems to be past, she is seen in company with a man who symbolizes the New South, the present. He is a labor foreman, head of a gang that is working on the streets of the town, physically changing the past. Finally, this man disappears, and Emily never leaves the house again. When she dies, her lover is discovered dead in the house, having been murdered many years before by his mistress. Apparently, the only way Emily could preserve a relationship was to kill its object. Faulkner has explained in an interview that Emily was shaped by her father's relentless selfishness. It was he who took away her opportunity for love and her capacity for it and left her with only the knowledge of taking rather than giving. When he dies, the town makes this observation: "We remembered all the young men her father had driven away, and we knew that with nothing left, she would have to cling to that which had robbed her, as people will."[5] Thus her father, one generation, in a sense killed her, or the best in her, the next generation, just as she actually kills the present in

4 *Ibid.*, 271–72.
5 *Ibid.*, 124.

the figure of Homer Barron. The story is clearly a forthright statement about the effect of past on present and the responsibility that follows the discovery of this effect.

The Sound and the Fury, generally considered to be Faulkner's masterpiece, is an early novel (1929), and I believe its theme to be the same as that of *A Fable* and *Requiem for a Nun*. The idea that Faulkner is a traditionalist bemoaning, in *The Sound and the Fury*, the passing of "the good old days" must be eradicated completely before one can understand it. The controlling and shaping generation, the image of the past, is represented in *The Sound and the Fury* by Mr. and Mrs. Compson and Uncle Maury. It is not the present corrupting the past which is here revealed, but the false values of the Old South which distort and destroy the present.

The absence of authority, the chaos visible here in the smallest matters, extends significantly to the world of moral order. There is no moral pattern, no inculcation of values. Instead of beliefs, Mrs. Compson has a pathetic allegiance to the idea of womanhood as she has conceived it by romantic illusion about the "Old South." For her, to be a "lady," to wear femininity as an ornament, is an end in itself. Some of the most pointed and effective irony is directed at Caroline Compson's unsatisfying dependence on her concept of herself as a Southern "lady." When Mrs. Compson reflects on the self-destruction of her son, she does so in these ironic terms:

> I dont know. What reason did Quentin have? Under God's heaven what reason did he have? It cant be simply to flout and hurt me. Whoever God is, He would not permit that. I'm a lady. You might not believe that from my offspring, but I am.[6]

Mrs. Compson's headaches are an outward manifestation of her internal sickness of character. She is totally impotent in

[6] William Faulkner, *The Sound and the Fury* (New York, 1929), 374.

all affairs, and her refuge is in self-pitying withdrawal. In a sense she is dead in life. She demonstrates an ineffectuality that Quentin inherits. Her influence is a negative one. The children know instinctively that their mother's sickness is symptom and symbol of her uselessness, to be turned on at will. Thus, Caddy can say to her: "You go upstairs and lay down, *so you can be sick*. I'll go get Dilsey."[7] (Italics are mine.)

Dilsey is the antithesis of Mrs. Compson in every way. The following scene is one of the keys to an understanding of the novel:

> "You sho you dont want nothin? Yo bottle still hot enough?"
> "You might hand me my Bible."
> "I give hit to you dis mawnin, befo I left."
> "You laid it on the edge of the bed. How long did you expect it to stay there?"
> Dilsey crossed to the bed and groped among the shadows beneath the edge of it and found the Bible, face down. She smoothed the bent pages and laid the book on the bed again. Mrs. Compson didn't open her eyes. Her hair and the pillow were the same color, beneath the wimple of the medicated cloth she looked like an old nun praying. "Dont put it there again," she said, without opening her eyes. "That's where you put it before. Do you want me to have to get out of bed to pick it up?"
> Dilsey reached the book across her and laid it on the broad side of the bed. "You cant see to read, noways," she said. "You want me to raise de shade a little?"
> "No. Let them alone. Go on and fix Jason something to eat."[8]

Ironically, Mrs. Compson is like "an old nun praying," but it is too dark for her to see the Bible. Dilsey must continually hand it to her, but she is not permitted to let in the light. In

[7] *Ibid.*, 78.
[8] *Ibid.*, 374–75.

Christian context the light and dark are symbolic, too. Dilsey, whose skin is dark, has become illuminated within by the light of awareness and belief. Mrs. Compson, whose face is the color of the pillow, willfully remains in the dark, and in darkness, both literally and metaphorically, cannot see the Bible. That Mrs. Compson is like a nun, unable to see the Bible, yet praying, is a significant commentary on her role in the novel. She is removed, cloistered from reality and living by adherence to the meaningless dogma of the code. She is unable to serve anybody in any way because she is devoid of that understanding that makes relationships meaningful.

In *The Sound and the Fury*, one of the supreme achievements is the realization of character. This is attained by a scrupulous attention to character consistency via point of view. Here the meaning never obtrudes into the sincerity of portrayal. Each character is recognizable by a distinctive outlook and vocabulary, so that if the character were not named we could still, on a second reading, identify him. The differences in the thinking of each character are accompanied by a peculiarity of style and vocabulary suitable to that thinking. Thus Benjy, who responds to experience purely in terms of sensory perception, is never permitted a rational or consecutive thought, he never draws a conclusion: "We ran up the steps and out of the bright cold, into the dark cold."[9] Jason talks as he thinks, in terms of the clichés by which a small-town shopkeeper lives. He always has the last word, the sardonic cheap joke, the sneering jibe. When his mother says, "I wish you'd take some aspirin," he replies, "Keep on wishing it . . . . It wont hurt you."[10] Quentin, who is confused and troubled, but at the same time sensitive and intelligent, is viewed in terms of the technique of interior monologue. He

[9] *Ibid.*, 6.
[10] *Ibid.*, 296.

is equipped with a large vocabulary and a complex sentence structure. So throughout, Faulkner adheres scrupulously to the fictional demands of the characters he has conceived. There is thus a variation of pace and a gain in dimension. The only point at which anything like a characteristic "Faulknerian style" is discoverable is at the opening of the fourth section.

> The day dawned bleak and chill. A moving wall of grey light out of the northeast which, instead of dissolving into moisture, seemed to disintegrate into minute and venomous particles, like dust that, when Dilsey opened the door of the cabin and emerged, needled laterally into her flesh precipitating not so much a moisture as a substance partaking of the quality of thin, not quite congealed oil.[11]

And here, too, this is no willful use of rhetoric, but a subtle shift from internal points of view to editorial omniscience. The people in *The Sound and the Fury* are real people and never sacrificed to a *Weltanschauung*.

The Sound and the Fury is a symbolic or at least a suggestive novel, with ranges of meaning not immediately apparent or expressed in forthright fashion. There are no "policy statements," serious pronouncements of belief, or pseudo-intellectual arguments. The "plot" is credible, the situations realistic. There is none of that artificial contrivance of plot or myth that characterizes *Requiem for a Nun, Intruder in the Dust,* or "The Bear."

The novel is rich in irony. Mrs. Compson provides the most striking examples of it. She claims to have brought her children up as Christians: one has become a whore, another a thief, and a third a suicide. Because we have access to the consciousness of each character, we can come to an awareness

[11] *Ibid.*, 330.

that the characters themselves never attain. No one but the
reader, for example, knows Quentin's thoughts just prior to
his death. The reader is able to make the connection between
those thoughts and the suicide itself, able to know that to the
last Quentin was thinking about the code which was all that
was offered to him as a system of belief—"no Compson ever
disappointed a lady." On learning that Quentin drowns himself, the reader is aware that Quentin is living, or rather dying,
in fulfillment of this doctrine, that he is, in an ironic sense,
not "disappointing" Mrs. Compson, who has, unknowingly
of course, prepared him for suicide. Mrs. Compson tells the
baby girl Quentin: "Poor little innocent baby,. . . You will
never know the suffering you have caused";[12] she is never
aware that the baby is a living accusation of herself. When she
says of Benjy, "It's a judgment on me. I sometimes wonder,"[13]
she is right in a sense that is beyond her understanding, just
as she is when she says, "I know I'm just a trouble and a burden to you."[14] These statements are part of her self-pity rather
than self-recrimination, but they strike chords of understanding in the reader.

Jason's section is also rich in irony. When he asks, "You
never resurrected Christ, did you?"[15] he is saying much more
than he means. Christ is presumably resurrected whenever
Christian belief is made a living reality, whenever the word is
made flesh. Mrs. Compson is dead in life, the hollow word.

It is by means of such understatement, incongruity, and implication that Faulkner is able to present a clear picture of the
success and failure of comparative approaches to the problems
of living. There is never any direct statement about "love and

12 *Ibid.*, 247.
13 *Ibid.*, 4.
14 *Ibid.*, 224.
15 *Ibid.*, 348.

honor and pride," never any sententiousness. Dilsey's humanity emerges through her actions. It is inconceivable that
Dilsey should say to anyone, "Believe," as Nancy does in a
later novel. But Dilsey's own belief is powerfully stated in
implicit terms in the course of the fiction. The "message" intended for the reader emerges by an implicit contrast of
values, not by any sermon that the author might have imposed on his narrative, as he did in several later novels.

The career of Sutpen in *Absalom, Absalom!* holds a fascina-
tion for Quentin, the modern man in search of a moral tradition, only because it provides a key to an understanding of
a whole society and its foundations. Like Flem Snopes in *The
Town*, Sutpen becomes accepted by society:

> . . . he was accepted; he obviously had too much money now to
> be rejected or even seriously annoyed any more. He accomplished
> this—got his plantation to running smoothly (he had an over-
> seer now; it was the son of that same sheriff who had arrested
> him at his bride-to-be's gate on the day of the betrothal) within
> ten years of the wedding, and now he acted his role too—a role
> of arrogant ease and leisure which, as the leisure and ease put
> flesh on him, became a little pompous.[16]

He has measured up to the demands of his peers, and, ironically, they are forced to recognize and acknowledge their
own parody. Sutpen's rise contains all the faults of the rise
of the plantation system: the total absence of human considerations; the ruthless and yet pointless goal of material ease;
a search for social dominance. William R. Poirier has particularly emphasized the inhuman character of Sutpen's rise. He
tells us that Sutpen pursues his design "with a complete in-
sensitivity to human character."[17] But these faults are not
newly found in Sutpen; they are part of what he copies.

[16] William Faulkner, *Absalom, Absalom!* (New York, 1936), 72.
[17] " 'Strange Gods' in Jefferson, Mississippi: Analysis of *Absalom, Absalom!*"

Yes, mad, yet not so mad. Because there is a practicality to viciousness: the thief, the liar, the murderer even, has faster rules than virtue ever has; why not madness too? If he was mad, it was only his compelling dream which was insane and not his methods.[18]

Sutpen's dream is the dream of all his contemporaries.

Quentin's interest in the Sutpen story is the result of his confusion as to his own moral role in society. To understand one's past is to better understand oneself. Quentin's grandfather was Sutpen's best, indeed only, friend, and thus the tie between Quentin and Sutpen is made closer. There is no doubt that to understand Quentin's interest in his past, one needs to be more fully acquainted with his present as it is revealed in *The Sound and the Fury.* The chaos of the present, the realization of his moral inadequacy, leads Quentin to seek some reason in the tradition: "Within the chaotic nature of Sutpen's history and Rosa's 'demonizing,' Quentin tries to find some human value adhering to what is apparently a representative anecdote of his homeland."[19] A look at the tradition does provide him with the terrible truth about his own place in time. Significantly enough, even Shreve, the remote, intellectual Canadian, becomes involved in the story, for it is really his story too. For the young it is quite clear that their shaping spirit rests in the past; Bon and Henry must look to their father for the cause of their problems. The four young men of the novel have in common their understanding of their own helplessness as victims of an amoral past, a past which irresponsibly disregarded the future effects of its actions and beliefs.

in *William Faulkner: Two Decades of Criticism* (ed. by Frederick J. Hoffman and Olga Vickery) (East Lansing, Mich., 1951), 222; hereafter cited as " 'Strange Gods.' "

18 *Absalom, Absalom!*, 166.

19 Poirier, " 'Strange Gods,' " *William Faulkner: Two Decades of Criticism*, 219.

Sutpen's poor-white background has its own nobility. There is a freedom and honesty in his early environment that is not simply part of a former, idyllic time in history, but one permanent aspect of a society which has another side, too. Sutpen's background is part of Faulkner's ideal conception of the possibilities of America, where all men are free, and all men have as much but no more than they need.

> . . . where he lived the land belonged to anybody and everybody and so the man who would go to the trouble and work to fence off a piece of it and say 'This is mine' was crazy; and as for objects, nobody had any more of them than you did because everybody had just what he was strong enough or energetic enough to take and keep, and only that crazy man would go to the trouble to take or even want more than he could eat or swap for powder and whiskey.[20]

During the Sutpens' wanderings, they come into contact with such a crazy system, the plantation system, where men own other men and devote themselves to a meaningless and useless existence. The first direct conflict with class occurs with two women in a carriage driven by a liveried Negro. Sutpen's sister refuses to get out of the road for it is her road as much as theirs, but power tells in this case, and the carriage rides down the Sutpen girl.

> [Sutpen sees] the carriage and the dust, the two faces beneath the parasols glaring down at his sister: then he was throwing vain clods of dirt after the dust as it spun on. He knew now, while the monkey-dressed nigger butler kept the door barred with his body while he spoke, that it had not been the nigger coachman that he threw at at all, that it was the actual dust raised by the proud delicate wheels, and just that vain.[21]

[20] *Absalom, Absalom!*, 221.
[21] *Ibid.*, 231.

This empty quality, the vanity of what Sutpen finds himself confronted by, is fundamental to an understanding of the novel's meaning. The flaw in Sutpen's design is the design itself. The plan is doomed from the start because it is by nature fallacious.

What Sutpen learns at the rich man's house, when he discovers his own innocence, is the incomprehensible, inexplicable nature of the class structure devised by man himself. Before he can give his message, Sutpen is told by the liveried Negro to go to the back of the house. It is as though he had come to tell the man that his house was on fire and then been told to go around to the back while it was burning down. The analogy is precise. The class system is based on abstractions, and in the service of abstractions the system itself breaks down. Sutpen is not angered by his experience; he is bewildered by it.

There is no doubt that Faulkner has succeeded in transmitting the sense of Sutpen's naïveté with surprising brilliance. The reader is almost amazed, as Quentin is amazed, by Sutpen's total unawareness of moral considerations. He is unable to see that the nature of the design determines its success.

> "You see, I had a design in my mind. Whether it was a good or a bad design is beside the point; the question is, Where did I make the mistake in it, what did I do or misdo in it, whom or what injure by it to the extent which this would indicate. I had a design. To accomplish it I should require money, a house, a plantation, slaves, a family—incidentally of course, a wife. I set out to acquire these, asking no favor of any man."[22]

Sutpen is convinced that only an error, a miscalculation, could have caused his defeat; he is unaware that the structure, how-

22 *Ibid.*, 263.

ever perfect, will wash away if built on sand. The story of
Sutpen subsequently consists of a series of fantastic illustrations of the conquest and use made of people as the "design"
is pieced together.

Poirier, in his essay on *Absalom, Absalom!* quotes the following passage from the novel: "The South would realize
that it was now paying the price for having erected its economic edifice not on the rock of stern morality but on the
shifting sands of opportunism and moral brigandage."[23] He
then goes on to say that "Faulkner, in these and other remarks
made in *Absalom, Absalom!*, gives full notice to the opinion
that the true nature of the plantation system and of Sutpen's
'design' was revealed negatively at the moment and in the act
of breakdown."[24] It seems impossible not to agree with Poirier.
The meaning of the novel is revealed in its form. The need to
re-examine the past is proof of Sutpen's failure, the failure of
Southern history. Sutpen is not immoral, he is amoral. Im-
morality at least implies the presense of an alternative. The
amoral person can perpetrate any evil because he is untroubled by a sense of guilt. The horror of Sutpen lies not in
his being the "demon" into which Rosa oversimplifies him,
but in his total unawareness of good and evil, in his want of
humanity. His is the story of all rapacious men who use human
beings as means rather than as ends. Sutpen is "on all fours
with the robber baron of the Gilded Age building a Renais-
sance palace on the banks of the Hudson."[25]

The breakdown of the Sutpen design, however, is a process
of self-affliction. In *Go Down, Moses,* Ike McCaslin utters the
following mental exclamation: "No wonder the ruined woods

---

23 *Ibid.*, 260.
24 " 'Strange Gods,' " *William Faulkner: Two Decades of Criticism*, 226.
25 Cleanth Brooks, "*Absalom, Absalom!*: The Definition of Innocence,"
Sewanee Review, Vol. LIX (Autumn, 1951), 547.

I used to know dont cry for retribution! he thought: The people who have destroyed it will accomplish its revenge."[26] The very process of destroying the woods makes man poorer. So in *Absalom! Absalom!* the acquisition of power and goods is an act of self-deprivation. To ignore human values is to deny oneself the supreme satisfaction of the humane life. Judith finds herself hopelessly confused about the meaning of life, just as Quentin is confused about his own role in the South's history. None of the young people in the novel have received any real set of values, any guidance, or any belief that is constant in the face of trouble and hardship. As Judith says:

> You get born and you try this and you dont know why only you keep on trying it and you are born at the same time with a lot of other people, all mixed up with them, like trying to, having to, move your arms and legs with strings only the same strings are hitched to all the other arms and legs and the others all trying and they dont know why either except that the strings are all in one another's way like five or six people all trying to make a rug on the same loom only each one wants to weave his own pattern into the rug; and it cant matter, you know that, or the Ones that set up the loom would have arranged things a little better, and yet it must matter because you keep on trying or having to keep on trying.[27]

Everyone in Sutpen's world is trying to weave his own pattern on the loom.

There are, however, a few instances in Faulkner's work where he shows everyone working at the same pattern. This might be said of the two Negro church meetings, one in *The Sound and the Fury* and the other at the end of *Soldiers' Pay*. The "loom" metaphor is a reference to the absence of harmony

26 *Go Down, Moses*, 364.
27 *Absalom, Absalom!*, 127.

35

and the presence of chaos. Judith's world has been all opposition, all exploitation. No thought has ever been given to her or Henry or Ellen for their own sakes. Only in a common respect for humanity can harmony, a single pattern, be achieved. Sutpen puts everybody at odds: Henry is forced to kill his brother; the Coldfields are used by Sutpen, and their unity is destroyed; Judith is denied marriage and family; Wash Jones is forced to kill his cherished granddaughter and her child. Sutpen is the very force and impulse of chaos. But it must never be forgotten that Sutpen is paradigm and symbol, victim as well as culprit. One must see Sutpen as an integral part of a system, a way of life. Quentin sees that he can find the key to his Southern past in the Sutpen history, a history that we all do well to examine. "The form of the novel itself insists that the act of placing Sutpen in the understandable context of human society and history is a continually necessary act, a neverending responsibility and an act of humanistic faith."[28]

Olga Vickery has said that "*As I Lay Dying* seems to be the one novel in which the author is in full control of his material."[29] If there is one such novel by Faulkner, it must surely be *Absalom, Absalom!* In no other novel does "control" strike one more forcibly on successive readings. There is no character who is not intensely involved in the Sutpen story, no one as detached as Peabody in *As I Lay Dying*. The extent to which the content is reflected in the technique is not equaled elsewhere. Cleanth Brooks thinks that it is Faulkner's best novel. Because it deals largely with states of mind reacting to events, rather than with the events themselves, *Absalom, Absalom!* is able to bear the burden of extended "rhetorical" statement

---

[28] Poirier, " 'Strange Gods,' " *William Faulkner: Two Decades of Criticism*, 243.

[29] "*As I Lay Dying*," *William Faulkner: Two Decades of Criticism*, 189.

and explanation. But the "speeches" are never Faulkner's or even Faulkner's in disguise. Each spokesman in the novel has his own particular viewpoint, each reveals himself in the process of examining others. It is this highly complex process of minds working in conjunction and opposition that gives the novel its masterful, highly wrought quality. Faulkner is doing several things at once. The story of Sutpen is revealed fragmentarily, details being uncovered as the examination continues. In this process the minds of the examiners are laid bare by a comparative method, a contrasting of their responses to history. The third over-all effect is one of balanced perspective; the reader is able to keep his distance. Only Quentin searches the past without a preconceived opinion of Sutpen; only he tries honestly to put aside the varieties of romanticism that dominate Rosa's and his father's view; and only Quentin comes to a full understanding of the real horror of Sutpen's amorality, a discovery which leaves him entirely on his own, to reassess, if he can, his role in time. Because of his control in handling his material here, Faulkner forces the reader to undertake the examination too. We must also balance the facts, as Quentin does. The result is that we come to Quentin's understanding: the horror of Sutpen's acts does not lie in Sutpen's defeat but in what he bequeathes to Judith and Henry, Bon and Quentin and Shreve, and to us.

The alternatives to Sutpen's course are absent here, which makes the novel more unified than it would otherwise be. We are, however, forced to an awareness of alternatives if we understand the novel. If Sutpen's failure and the suffering he causes stem from the absence of human values, the absence of human emotion, and a complete disregard for the consequences of his acts, it is not difficult to see the deliberate implications. *Absalom, Absalom!* is a stronger work because Faulkner does not try to explain how we should achieve these alternatives. But because he has not been explicit, Faulkner has misled some critics. Edgar W. Whan has tried so hard to prove that Faulkner is writing a "Gothic" novel in *Absalom, Absalom!* that he has been led to ignore its meaning.

> To say that life is meaningless, that man is helpless against the fates, is one thing, but when over this conception hovers the knowledge that these elements have been met before, that there is the Gothic chill which rises delicately from the very formal qualities themselves, then the idea partakes of horror. Man is not even capable of tragedy, he is only the victim of a practical joke.[30]

This is only one of many statements to the same effect. Those who are well acquainted with Faulkner's work know that he has never represented man as the helpless victim of a hostile cosmos. To say this would be to destroy greatly his whole outlook. The world is so designed that meaning must be found or made by man. Man creates his own evil when he chooses death, of one kind or another, over life. Critics have too often presented Faulkner as his own worst example of human helplessness and failure. Sutpen is not the victim of a pointless cosmic irony. He plants the seeds of his own destruction very carefully. Mr. Whan's kind of reading turns the novel inside out. It is not that the story is designed to provide Faulkner with "Gothic," horrific effect. Certainly there is horror, and Faulkner wishes us to experience it because he does not believe that it is a necessary and inevitable condition of being human. He wishes to convey precisely the nature and origin of the horrific. The degeneration of the race into Jim Bonds is assured as long as the system which Sutpen apes is reestablished or survives.

Light in August (another early novel, 1932) reiterates these values in the story of Lena Grove. Lena thinks that people are

[30] *"Absalom, Absalom!* as Gothic Myth," *Perspective,* Vol. III (Autumn, 1950), 201.

very kind: *"Behind her the four weeks, the evocation of far, is a peaceful corridor paved with unflagging and tranquil faith and peopled with kind and nameless faces and voices."*[31] It is significant that her belief conflicts with everything that we have learned from other sources about the people in the novel. Her belief is a clue to her own character; from her own goodness she judges others. We know, when Lena says that Mrs. Armstid is being kind by giving her money, that Martha Armstid is being good without being kind, as her husband rightly judges.[32] She gives Lena money but will not appear at breakfast to say a kind word. Perhaps, however, kindness is as much a part of how the act is viewed as of the act itself. Certainly Lena and Byron move in exactly the same world as Joe Christmas, yet it is paradoxically a very different world for them. Together they represent the ideal alternative to the world of chaos in which Christmas moves. They are a contrast, not as is generally thought to Joe Christmas, but to the society which molds him and then rejects him. That is why they never confront him. In a sense it would be pointless for Christ to seek acceptance at the hands of those already good. Until she finds Byron (through her faith), Lena finds no more acceptance than Christmas. Although people help her, they will never accept her, an unwed mother, and they judge her as self-righteously as we would expect. Byron does accept her, however, and so together they represent the only hope for the future of the race. Theirs will be a union based on love, a love which eradicates the evil of the past. They are *"The good stock peopling in tranquil obedience to it the good earth; from these hearty loins without hurry or haste descending mother and daughter."*[33]

[31] William Faulkner, *Light in August* (New York, 1932), 4.
[32] *Ibid.*, 10.
[33] *Ibid.*, 384.

In many ways, *Light in August* is Faulkner's greatest achievement. At least it is so by the author's definition. Faulkner thought that the ambitious failure is better than the unambitious success. *Light in August* is a great failure. It does not have the form, the order, the unity, or the intensity of *The Sound and the Fury*. But I think that it is more searching in its universality, and the alternatives it presents are stronger because they are not so specifically religious. Faulkner is not here ordering us to "believe," but telling us to look at the wondrous complexities of our world with fresh eyes. Mary Cooper Robb has said, "It is avoiding the issue he [Faulkner] raises if a reader sees only the South in his books, and thinks his people are only Southerners with consequently only Southern problems to solve."[34] Faulkner has made a similar observation: "He's not really writing about his environment, he's simply telling a story about human beings in the terms of environment . . . . The novelist is talking about people, about man in conflict with himself, his fellows, or his environment."[35]

The universality of *Light in August* is the source of its power. The characters are individuals and types at the same time. If Joe Christmas were called Smith, his role would be just as recognizable. He does achieve a personal grandeur and a vivid reality; he does become a truly tragic hero.[36] The fact that the characters here are fully realized, are not allegorical, is an undeniable strength and leads to an inevitable contrast with *A Fable*.

[34] *William Faulkner: An Estimate of His Contribution to the American Novel*, 10.

[35] *Nagano*, 157.

[36] Joe Christmas has been thoroughly examined as a tragic hero in a very convincing study by John L. Longley, "Joe Christmas: The Hero in the Modern World," *Virginia Quarterly Review*, Vol. XXXIII (Spring, 1957), 233–49.

Light in August is almost identically the same as *A Fable* in its themes. It contains a Christ-figure, a past-dominated figure, a noninvolved believer, and so on. None of these figures in *A Fable* is seen, however, in his natural environment. There, Faulkner has moved away from the creativity of his imagination towards the contrivances of his intellect. The corporal as Christ, accompanied by twelve companions, is a less-human figure than Joe Christmas. In the one novel we are *told* what to think; in the other our attitudes naturally develop in response to vividly drawn people and events. *Light in August* reiterates its themes by a series of different dramatic scenes, acted by different examples of the same types. *A Fable* pores over the same themes through the contrived ponderings of unreal characters. The emphasis in the later novel is on the positive, the solution, while in the earlier it is action as metaphor that gives birth to the theme. The meaning of *Light in August* is found not so much in what people say or think, as in what they do. The reader's mind remembers vivid pictures: the boy Christmas falling in a faint for want of food while holding the catechism he is pointlessly forced to memorize; the dead Joanna beheaded like an ancient English queen; the baby Christmas eating toothpaste behind the closet curtain while the dietitian is raped on the bed; the machine-like Grimm lunging at Christmas in the final gesture of total repudiation. These pictures stay with us. It is the artist's imagination communicating with our own. In *A Fable*, people say and think more than they do. The figures are speculative, not dynamic, and we are not inclined to be impressed by the long and tedious ramifications of these wooden models. There are no long speeches in *Light in August*; there is no rhetoric, and there is very little description. What description there is, is vivid and precise: "The sharp and brittle crack and clatter of its weathered and ungreased wood and metal is slow and terrific: a series of dry sluggish reports carrying for a half mile across the hot still pinewiney silence of the August afternoon."[37]

Joseph Christmas symbolizes the cause and demonstrates the effect of man's failing. His dual coloring is an ironic emblem for the divided society in which he moves, a society which will not throw over its pointless bigotry (pointless because it is not even certain that Christmas is a Negro) and recognize its common humanity. Christmas' mixed blood also symbolizes the good and evil that is found in the marshal in *A Fable*. In that novel, the people insist that God act as the devil. They bring evil upon themselves. Joe Christmas is likewise forced to be evil by a society which will not let him be good. He enters the Negro church as Satan and that is what he has become. Man perverts the best in himself continually. Joe Christmas is a victim of society, and consequently an image of society itself. But Lena Grove and Byron Bunch are society too, and Faulkner, true to his belief in man, ends his novel with them.

The Unvanquished and *Sartoris* are not great novels. They lack the grand prose, the complex and ironic organization, the elaborate and profound analysis of states of mind that characterize the above work. Faulkner's genius in handling individual human psychology at the same time as he creates a symbolic role for his character, as with Joe Christmas, is not obvious here, nor is his bewildering mastery of language as it shifts from thundering rhetoric to exquisite lyricism. But these works are important because they touch on themes, are indeed built around themes, that are to persist and reappear most strongly twenty and thirty years later.

In *The Unvanquished* the fortunes of the Sartoris family during the Civil War provide a theme constant enough to

[37] *Light in August*, 5.

give unity to the collection of stories. Rosa Millard, Colonel John Sartoris, and Bayard Sartoris are the principal characters in this rather simple and unprofound drama. I am principally concerned with only one of the stories—the last. "Odor of Verbena" provides a point and resolution to the chapters preceding it. It is very important to keep in mind that this last story was added when the collection was published. Before this addition there was nothing to signify that the stories were anything but a handful of not very striking tributes to the undefeated spirit of a people who had lost a bitter war.

In a sense, Rosa Millard's heroism arises out of her humanistic convictions which she acts upon while questioning her first principles. She is ready to admit that she is wrong, even when compelled by circumstances to act forcefully. Faulkner is careful to save her from the charge of self-righteousness, a sin which, it would seem from some of his writing, he considers to be the unforgivable one. The stories which deal with "Granny" and the revenge for her murder have the quality of folk stories. Although engaging, they do not make any substantial contribution to an understanding of Faulkner's work. The last story, however, is surprising. It is such a rejection of all the tributes that constitute the stories which precede it that it seems to give to the title of the volume an ironic new dimension.

Bayard, in this last story, becomes "The Sartoris." Prior to this we have seen him only as a child, living in a world dominated by the image of his father. The whole countryside pays tribute to the legendary courage and daring of Colonel Sartoris. In "Odor of Verbena" we learn from Bayard's cousin and stepmother, Drusilla, that life has become cheap because of the war. She tells him that ten or twenty lives are worth nothing; that courage and honor are more important. Bayard, however, has his own interpretation of honor. He "became a man and went to college to learn law."[38] His study of law is in itself significant and implies a rejection of the entire code that reigned in his tradition. Bayard returns from college to face Redmond, his father's killer. He is urged by Drusilla to kill, by his aunt Jenny to hide. He has his own method, however, of coping with killers. His own intrinsic courage forces him to face Redmond, but he does so unarmed, with no intention of killing. Faulkner, in a process of recapitulation, painstakingly explains that John Sartoris had been by no means lily-white in his dealings with Redmond—it is difficult if not impossible to know where to lay the blame for the killing. Bayard has once in his life avenged the death of a relative by murder. He did what was expected of him by the code of his tradition. In this new instance he rejects the code, finding his own solution to the problem of retribution. He faces Redmond unarmed. In this way, by a kind of passive yet positive resistance, he brings about the end of the feud with a finality not achieved by the killing prescribed in the code. Thus Bayard makes a break with his past.

In *The Unvanquished* the last story provides the meaning for the whole collection. Ringo's explanation of Rosa Millard's death becomes understandable. "It wasn't him or Ab Snopes either that kilt her," Ringo said. "It was them mules. That first batch of mules we got for nothing."[39] The moral seems to be that a disregard for social law and order, regardless of its noble motives, inevitably leads to evil consequences. The ends do not justify the means. Bayard goes to college dedicated to the principle that means are all important. It is this discovery of ethics, this assertion that Northerners like the Burdens are human beings too and cannot be killed out

[38] William Faulkner, *The Unvanquished* (New York, 1938), 251.
[39] *Ibid.*, 211.

of hand, as John Sartoris killed them, that raises Bayard to the level of hero. It is he who is unvanquished. It is the dominance of the best of Rosa Millard in him, rather than the worst, that gives point to the new holder of the title, "The Sartoris." He is the promise of a new generation of understanding. Bayard thus provides the positive view which can be found in all the early novels. True, here as in *Mosquitoes*, there is little philosophy, little that is explicit. The values that are presented as alternatives are not clearly evolved or asserted. Yet Bayard does provide a paradigm of behavior by his adherence to a fundamental respect for human life and dignity, just as Gordon in *Mosquitoes* rejects façade and pursues the underlying realities that he is equipped to perceive.

Sartoris is about the return of a war hero. The war here, however, and the problems of a young Bayard Sartoris grow not only out of contemporary chaos but from a traditional absence of values. For close readers of Faulkner the following comment by George M. O'Donnell must always be a surprise: "The Sartorises act traditionally; that is to say, they act always with an ethically responsible will. They represent vital morality, humanism."[40]

The very history of the Sartorises is under indictment here, and the presence of a predatory Snopes is not the cause but the symptom of social failure on the part of the tradition. In *The Town*, Faulkner refers to the last days of the Civil War as "that desperate twilight of 1864–65 when more people than men named Snopes had to choose not survival with honor but simply between empty honor and almost as empty survival."[41] And this is not a new view. As early as 1929, Faulkner produced the following dialogue on the Civil War:

[40] "Faulkner's Mythology," *William Faulkner: Two Decades of Criticism*, 50.

[41] *The Town*, 42.

Old Bayard shook the ash from his cigar. "Will," he said, "what the devil were you folks fighting about, anyhow?"

"Bayard," old man Falls answered, "be damned ef I ever did know."[42]

Add to this what we know of Colonel Sartoris' ethics from *The Unvanquished,* and it becomes clear that in spite of all the glamour and bravado of Sartoris exploits, Faulkner sees through to the underlying moral weaknesses of the old Southern position.

As in *Soldiers' Pay,* the indigent Negroes are here revealed as morally superior to their white masters. One of the Sartoris retainers asks the question, "What us niggers want ter be free fer, anyhow? Ain't we got ez many white folks now ez we kin suppo't?"[43] The Negroes are supposed to take their standards from their "betters," and the Sartorises have failed to live up to their responsibilities and obligations. The most revealing dialogue in *Sartoris* takes place between Simon and "The Sartoris":

"Do you mean to tell me you took charge of money belonging to other people, and then went and loaned it to somebody else?"

"You does de same thing ev'ry day," Simon answered. "Ain't lendin' money yo' main business?"[44]

Old Bayard has himself introduced the system of finance capitalism into the South; it is fitting that many novels later Flem Snopes should take over the presidency of it. The gap between Sartoris and Snopes is not as large as O'Donnell would have us believe. The moral superiority of the very people who have been the slaves is further pointed out by the portrayal of the Negro whom young Bayard visits on Christmas. He refuses to

[42] William Faulkner, *Sartoris* (New York, 1929), 227.
[43] *Ibid.,* 83.
[44] *Ibid.,* 233.

46

be bribed away from his fireside on such a day by any amount of money.

Irving Howe has commented on the young Bayard's unfortunate heritage: "This similarity of character [between the two Bayards] suggests that the young Bayard's self-destructiveness is not merely a personal dilemma, but is rooted in the very past from which he now feels cut off."[45] Bayard's problems as an inheritor of an inhuman past are underlined by the picture of the children of the present, the "Bayards" of the future. Vergil Beard, who writes Snopes's "love" letters, is most fond of shooting singing birds and squirting acid into people's eyes. Little Belle is continually sacrificed by her mother's promiscuity and final divorce and remarriage. The world that young Bayard returns to is peopled by characters of moral incompetence, lustful impulses, self-interest, and greed. It is in this novel that the first mention is made of a man who makes money by tying mules to the railroad tracks. It is little wonder that Bayard is unable to either join the society, after the war experience, or find any alternative to it in a valueless tradition characterized by glamorous opportunism. Death is his only answer, and his death is a virtual suicide.

After the death of his grandfather, young Bayard significantly makes two visits. Freed from the bonds of his tradition, he turns to the classless McCallums who live away from town, and therefore away from the false concerns of society. They live an almost idyllic existence in the woods, taming nature without destroying, surrounded with a profusion of food and living in family harmony and moral purity. On leaving the McCallums, Bayard visits a cabin where Negroes live in extreme squalor, barely subsisting on the land. These Negroes are surely meant as a contrast to the primitive richness of the McCallums, the one family a product of the class system, as

[45] *William Faulkner: A Critical Study* (New York, 1952), 29.

it was run by Sartorises and their kind, and the other family indicating the joy and plenty of a life lived in harmony with men and nature, man taking from his environment no more than he needs. This novel, like the others considered here, posits human values against abstractions, morality against might-as-right, humility in the face of the God-made, and love as the only possible means of achieving a satisfactory and harmonious life.

CHAPTER III

"The Bear"

"That was symbolism"

The long short story "The Bear" illustrates perfectly the change of emphasis which has characterized Faulkner's work since 1948. "The Bear" is in many ways the turning point in the work of Faulkner, the signpost which indicates his change of direction from the creation of myth to the construction of discourse, from the play of imagination to the exercise of ratiocination. Both by its internal structure and by the history of its composition, "The Bear" reveals the tendency in Faulkner to explicit statement, to rhetoric, to monologue, and to sententiousness. By examining the theme of the destruction of the wilderness and by critically analyzing the values that end it and survive it, we will see that Faulkner has in this work been constant to his simple, humanistic outlook. But an examination of the method will show that Faulkner has adopted here the characteristics of allegory and essay and that several participants in the action are emblems rather than characters—a situation which never occurs in the work of the previous two decades.

The earliest version of "The Bear" (1935) shows none or few of these later characteristics. For one thing it is not called "The Bear," but "Lion," the dog who hunts the bear. This in itself is worth noting. Old Ben, the bear of the later story, is a manifestation of the essential wilderness; the hunting of him is a ritual, in which all the participants have set roles to play like actors on a stage. In 1935, however, "Lion" was simply a very good hunting story about Boon Hogganbeck and Lion, told by a boy whose role in the drama was minimal. Nor, in the early story, was that boy the same as the later one. He was Quentin, an already well-established Faulkner character, taking part merely as a member of that Mississippi community. And Uncle Ike is a character conceived of as an already old man. Only later, in *Go Down, Moses,* is Ike's entire hunting history revealed, and he is substituted as the youthful acolyte of the hunt. We may again well ask why this change was necessary. In "The Bear," Ike clearly indicates that he sees himself as a chosen figure in God's scheme. There seems to be a clear parallel here to the Isaac of Genesis, with whom God made a covenant about people and land. And Faulkner's Isaac, like his prototype, loves hunting and favors the one who can bring him venison in his old age. Ike McCaslin, in "Delta Autumn," when, as an old man, he lies in his tent and sends forth his nephews to kill deer is meant to recall the son of Abraham. These changes in the later versions are powerful indications of the new seriousness and intensity with which Faulkner seeks to present his theme, and they serve to illustrate that theme itself which clearly has to do with man's relationship to man, his environment, and God. The shift of point of view from first person to omniscient author between 1935 and 1942 underlines Faulkner's growing desire to keep a closer control over the presentation of his material and reveals the need for a device which will enable the author to analyze and comment on his own fiction.

There are other indications of this movement to the structure of allegory. The style itself has become, in "The Bear," more elaborate, rhetorical, and involved. Let us compare, for instance, the opening paragraph of "Lion" with the same subject as treated in "The Bear":

A good part of the lives of dogs—I mean hunting dogs, bear and deer dogs—is whiskey. That is, the men who love them, who hunt hard the hard-hunting and tireless and courageous dogs, drink hard too. I know certainly that the best, the finest talk about dogs which I have heard took place over a bottle or two or three bottles maybe, in the libraries of town houses and the offices of plantation houses or, better still, in the camps themselves; before the burning logs on hearths when there were houses, or before the high blazing of nigger-fed wood before stretched and earth-pegged tarpaulins when there were not. So this story might just as well begin with whiskey too.[1]

This became:

There was always a bottle present, so that it would seem to him that those fine fierce instants of heart and brain and courage and wiliness and speed were concentrated and distilled into that brown liquor which not women, not boys and children, but only hunters drank, drinking not of the blood they spilled but some condensation of the wild immortal spirit, drinking it moderately, humbly even, not with the pagan's base and baseless hope of acquiring thereby the virtues of cunning and strength and speed but in salute to them. Thus it seemed to him on this December morning not only natural but actually fitting that this should have begun with whiskey.[2]

In the first the narrative is direct, colloquial, and spoken from the consciousness of the "I"; in the other there is an attempt to seek out and to worry to the surface all the psychological implications—the author speaking for the boy, explaining, probing, using syntactical extension, inversion, and oratorical devices to create an almost exalted epical effect.

[1] William Faulkner, "Lion," *Harper's Magazine*, Vol. CLXXII (December, 1935), 67.
[2] *Go Down, Moses*, 192.

In "Lion," Faulkner describes the behavior of the dogs after the death of the bear in this way: "It was as though Old Ben, even dead and harmless out there in the yard, was a more potent force than they were alive without Lion to lead them, and they knew it."[3] In *Go Down, Moses* it has been subtly changed: "It was as if the old bear, even dead there in the yard, was a more potent terror still than they could face without Lion between them."[4] All suggestions of comparison between bear and dogs have been removed, and instead the suggestion is that Lion is a shield from the primitive power of the bear rather than a leader of lesser dogs. In other words, he has become more a symbol and less just another hunting dog.

Perhaps more than anything else the fourth chapter indicates things to come. Here Ike McCaslin and his cousin Cass indulge in a forthright debate about the moral needs and the moral answers which exist for a white McCaslin in the early twentieth century in Mississippi. We do not need, at this point, to concern ourselves with the details of that verbal struggle. Suffice it to say that it is perfectly illustrative of fictional techniques that were to become more predominant in Faulkner's later writing, and if any reader is surprised by the discussions in *Requiem for a Nun* or by the dialogue in *A Fable*, let him reread the McCaslin debate in "The Bear." The omission of the family-history episode from *The Big Woods* version would seem to imply that in the eyes of the editors, perhaps even for Faulkner himself, such an episode has no place in the unity of the hunting story as a hunting story.

The principal difficulty in interpreting "The Bear" is to discover the unity between the section on the McCaslin family history and the hunting story. But it would seem that to dis-

[3] "Lion," *Harper's Magazine*, Vol. CLXXII (December, 1935), 75.
[4] *Go Down, Moses*, 247.

cover this unity is possible only when each section is understood separately. I believe that the story up to the death of
Sam Fathers has a profound symbolic meaning.

A close examination of "The Bear" will reveal that it is
Faulkner's intention here to turn legend into allegory. Faulkner begins by telling us that "there was a man and a dog too
this time. Two beasts, counting Old Ben, the bear, and two
men, counting Boon Hogganbeck."[5] Faulkner would seem to
imply, as early as his first two sentences, that Old Ben is not
really a beast and Boon is not really a man. The word "counting" can be explained only in this way. What is Ben if he is
not really a beast? He is the wilderness itself. He is a legend,
a long one: "The long legend of corn-cribs broken down and
rifled, of shoats and grown pigs and even calves carried bodily
into the woods and devoured."[6] He is a ferocious force devoid
of malice, but unbeatable. He is "an anachronism . . . out of an
old dead time."[7] Sam Fathers, half-Indian, half-Negro, self-
dedicated to the woods, knows that Ben is without sentiment
and dismisses contemptuously the story that Ben takes care of
the younger bears. "He don't care no more for bears than he
does for dogs or men either."[8] Ben, the "chief bear," is an
essence, a distillation of the power and spirit and fate of the
wilderness.

What is Boon if he is not really a man? He is a child, with
the mind of a child in his man's body; he "was four inches over
six feet; he had the mind of a child, the heart of a horse, and
little hard shoe-button eyes without depth or meanness or

[5] William Faulkner, *The Big Woods* (New York, 1955), 11. My prelim-
inary discussion of "The Bear" depends upon reading it solely as a hunting
story. It therefore seems appropriate to refer to this collection of Faulkner's
hunting stories.
[6] *Ibid.*, 12–13.
[7] *Ibid.*, 13.
[8] *Ibid.*, 18.

generosity or viciousness or gentleness or anything else."[9] He is childlike in the face of the complexities of civilization. With a gun he is useless. Whoever finally would shoot the bear, "It would not be Boon. He had never hit anything bigger than a squirrel that anybody ever knew, except the Negro woman that day when he was shooting at the Negro man."[10]

Lion is the wild mongrel dog who is afraid of nothing. He is a mixture of many breeds, "part mastiff, something of airedale, and something of a dozen other strains probably."[11] His color is frequently emphasized: "and all over that strange color like a blued gun-barrel."[12] It is also the color of Boon's beard: "That blue stubble on his face like the filings from a new gun-barrel."[13] The dog, too, is completely without sentiment. It appears only as a relentless force, without feeling, as for instance when it "hurled itself tirelessly against the door and dropped back and leaped again. It never made any sound and there was nothing frenzied in the act but only a cold and grim indomitable determination."[14] This absence of feeling, of attachment, of "meanness or generosity or gentleness or viciousness,"[15] is replaced by a fixed purposefulness that is derived from nothing. It is merely a major element in the natural phenomenon which is the dog. There is only

> the blue hide beneath which the muscles flinched or quivered to no touch since the heart which drove blood to them loved no man and nothing, standing as a horse stands yet different from a horse which infers only weight and speed while Lion inferred not only courage and all else that went to make up the will and desire to

9 *Ibid.*, 50.
10 *Ibid.*, 59.
11 *Ibid.*, 40.
12 *Ibid.*, 40.
13 *Ibid.*, 55.
14 *Ibid.*, 39.
15 *Ibid.*, 62.

pursue and kill, but endurance, the will and desire to endure *beyond all imaginable limits of flesh* in order to overtake and slay.[16] (Italics are mine.)

It is not amiss here to note the similarity in some respects between Lion and Boon. Boon's eyes, too, are devoid of "meanness or generosity or gentleness or viciousness." Boon's beard is the same color as Lion's body, and Boon, in the course of the story, proves that he has limitless bravery. He finds himself drawn to Lion and becomes the servant of the dog.

> It was as if Lion were a woman—or perhaps Boon was the woman. That was more like it—the big, grave, sleepy-seeming dog which, as Sam Fathers said, cared about no man and no thing; and the violent, insensitive, hard-faced man with his touch of remote Indian blood and the mind almost of a child.[17]

These are the similarities. A little later we will go into the differences.

In addition to Old Ben, Boon, and the dog, there are two other principal characters in this drama. Sam Fathers, like the bear, is an anachronism. He, too, is part of the wilderness, part of its very spirit and essence. He must live in it. He understands it, loves it, is bound by humility in the face of its natural wonders. Part Indian and part Negro, he combines the best of the innocence of both races. Civilization has not touched Sam Fathers. He is the human equivalent of Old Ben. His function in the story, as a figure representing the best of the past, is to be the finest possible teacher for Ike McCaslin.

When Ike is ten years old, he graduates from hunting rabbits and squirrels to hunting deer and bear. His entire tutelage is under Sam. Old Ben becomes for the boy the object of all hunting, the principal figure in the whole wilderness drama,

16 *Ibid.*, 61–62.
17 *Ibid.*, 43.

which grows to be the dominant theme in his life: "It loomed and towered in his dreams before he ever saw the unaxed woods where it left its crooked print, shaggy, tremendous, red-eyed, not malevolent but just big."[18] The boy dedicates himself to the woods, is baptized in blood as a hunter, and learns humility and "love and pity for all which lived and ran and then ceased to live in a second in the very midst of splendor and speed";[19] he even breaks the bonds of time and space to become part of the wilderness.

> He stood for a moment—a child, alien and lost in the green and soaring gloom of the markless wilderness. Then he relinquished completely to it. It was the watch and the compass. He was still tainted. He removed the linked chain of the one and the looped thong of the other from his overalls and hung them on a bush and leaned the stick beside them and entered it.[20]

These are the principal characters in "The Bear"; among them they provide its entire meaning. The meaning of the story is difficult to reach, yet the urge to examine it is compelling; as a hunting story it has little to do with hunting. Much space and time are devoted to minute descriptions of characters, who, except for Ike, never become real. They have no depth. They are clearly seen, but only for a moment. The bear is obviously no ordinary bear, just as the dog is no ordinary dog—they are forthright symbols. Since Old Ben is called "an anachronism, out of an old dead time," it does not require very much imagination to sense that in a way we have here a symbol, not only of the wilderness-past, the prehistoric past, but of all history, because the wilderness in its turn is merely a metaphor; it is whatever is past, all dead time. Therefore, an examination of how the bear is killed should reveal some-

18 *Ibid.*, 13.
19 *Ibid.*, 133.
20 *Ibid.*, 29.

thing of the nature of that progress which constitutes change. The death of the bear is a parable of mutation.

Two creatures, Lion and Boon, are responsible for Ben's death. Their relationship is important. Lion, as we have seen, is entirely without sentiment. He acts in relentless pursuit, never gives ground, is unresponsive to affection. He is, in fact, nothing recognizable at all, except that because of his function and with his gun-barrel-blue color and his brute strength, he seems to symbolize the undeviating force of destructive change. The mixture of breeds, mentioned before, further indicates the complexities and divisions of progress and makes more rigid the creature's allegorical nature, since it thus becomes less recognizable as a dog. It is mechanical in its characteristics, thus emphasizing the relentless, inevitable and automatic nature of change. The bear must die, the dog must kill—this is as much a part of the order of things as the rising and setting of the sun.

Boon requires more analysis, since he embodies a dichotomy. As we see most clearly from *A Fable*, Faulkner demands a positive morality, achieved by a conscious choice following an awareness of evil. There is nothing to evoke pride in the knowledge of innate innocence; it is the other kind of innocence consequent upon absolution from guilt that enables man to climb back into Eden. Boon never can make this ascent. He is immature man, a symbol for the infancy of both the individual and the race—Boon is part Indian and part white. The Indian part of him is presumably the primitive innocent. Within the figure of Boon, Faulkner has crystallized his view of the human plight. Boon, man, is a pathetic fallen Adam, unable, after the discovery of evil, to cope with and combat it and, therefore, unable to regain his former innocence.

Boon's immaturity is symbolized by his inability to cope

with civilization. On his trip to Memphis he is unable to resist the lure of the tavern, and it is in the city, and presumably because of the city, that he gets drunk. Ike, in contrast, refuses even a lemonade, and no mention is ever made of Ike's eating city-bought food. Clearly, therefore, the indictment is of Boon, not of the city, for by yielding to its evils, the man sanctions and substantiates them. Within civilization Ike remains untouched—it is he who is responsible for Boon's return to the woods, the return to purity.

Another instance of Boon's futility in the face of "progress" is his conduct in the final scene of "The Bear," present in all versions. He is found by Ike

> hammering furiously at something on his lap. What he hammered with was the barrel of his dismembered gun, what he hammered at was the breech of it. The rest of the gun lay scattered about him in a half-dozen pieces while he bent over the piece on his lap his scarlet and streaming walnut face, hammering the disjointed barrel against the gun-breech with the frantic abandon of a madman. He didn't even look up to see who it was.[21]

Relationships with human beings forgotten, he is drawn frantically into the overwhelming whirlpool of mechanical progress. It is interesting to note how confusing this last scene is to the critics. It has caused much puzzlement and controversy, arising from the seeming inconsistency between an earlier sympathetic portrayal of Boon and a final critical one. If one understands the symbolic nature of Boon, all else falls into place. The most pertinent question with regard to the meaning of the climax of the story, the death of the bear, the "piece of statuary," is why Boon is part of that tableau, why Boon is given the task of killing the bear.

History, the past, Old Ben, can never escape change, sym-

[21] *Ibid.*, 97.

bolized by Lion. This is the inevitable pattern and order of the universe.[22] Although Boon cannot cope with progress, neither can he resist it. What other meaning is there in his love, almost sexual, of the dog Lion? Man is, by his nature, dedicated to change. Man plays a part in change; he must put his seal on the death of the bear. But we have seen what kind of man Boon is. He is essentially weak, incompetent, and bewildered. Up to the present, as Faulkner sees it, man has helped bring about changes without the ability to cope with the inevitable new circumstances. Boon is helpless in civilization, yet symbolically he is responsible for his presence there. Thus does Faulkner censure man for his inadequacies in the face of evils of his own making. Sam dies when Ben dies. Sam, the good and innocent, the "taintless" man, is destroyed by the surviving incompetent side of man.[23] It should be noticed, too, that in the killing of the bear, Boon becomes marked, permanently scarred. The past does leave its mark on the present. Man cannot get away unscathed.

Into this story comes Ike, the specific human protagonist in the midst of the abstract allegory, who throughout is merely an observer, the student, trained by the pure man, Sam. Ike, being human, is not perfect; "only Sam and Old Ben and the mongrel Lion were taintless and incorruptible."[24] Ike learns love and pity and pride and humility. Parentless, that is without a past directly forced upon him, he is able to stand back and observe objectively the values of past and present. Thus he does not kill the bear, but he is the only witness to its

[22] At Nagano, Faulkner made this comment: "No, I don't hold to the idea. I don't hold to the idea of a return. That once the advancement stops then it dies. It's got to go forward and we have got to take along with us all the rubbish of our mistakes and our errors." *Nagano*, 77–78.

[23] My interpretation of the symbology here is borne out by the literal events. There is a strong suggestion that Boon killed Sam at the latter's request. *Go Down, Moses*, 253–54.

[24] *The Big Woods*, 11.

destruction. He has the opportunity to kill the bear but is outside the pageant of its demise. In the same way, it is he alone who is able to see Boon's final frustration with gun and squirrels. In the version we are discussing now, his visit to the gum tree is the last he will make to the wilderness. He goes there "one more time" to get one more lesson. He sees that it is Boon, so often mistaken as a noble participant in the drama, who has finally and completely introduced the concept of "mine" into the new world.

This is the story of the hunting of Old Ben and one way of looking at its meaning. It would appear that Ike is full of promise for redressing the wrongs resulting from the incompetence of such as Boon, since he is equipped with the best of the old values, the values mentioned by Faulkner at Stockholm. It is in this way that the connection between the section devoted to Ike and his family and the rest of the story is made clear.

We see man, immature and unaware of his responsibility, destroy the past and introduce changes which he cannot understand or shape to his satisfaction. But Faulkner is not a satirist—if he makes a critical commentary on man, we must expect that he will show us an affirmative side, too. The abstract observations embodied in Boon and Ben and Lion and Sam are converted by the McCaslin section into specific problems and answers for the individual in a real community of men. The implications of the hunting episode would appear to be clear enough, and in earlier years Faulkner would have let them stand alone, but here, as in the other later novels, he feels it necessary to accentuate and spell out the pattern of conduct that man must follow. He does this by taking the potential in Ike and submitting it to one of two possible destinies, the other being there by implication, noted by its absence. Both are part of "The Bear" in *Go Down, Moses*, and we may turn to "Delta Autumn" for a completion of the study of Ike.

Inserted into the plot structure related earlier, and prior to the final section, is a chapter which gives the family history of McCaslin and Ike's response to the facts revealed in that history. The whole is in the form of a debate between Ike and his cousin McCaslin. Ike has been brought up by his cousin. From the fictional point of view this is important because Faulkner's heroes often have doubtful parentage or are brought up by people other than their parents. This is the case with Joe Christmas, who as a result is without moral identity; it is true of the corporal in *A Fable*, who meets his father only at death; and it is true of Ike. This alone, then, sets Ike a little apart from his tradition and makes credible the shock with which he discovers the nature of that tradition.

The line begins with Carothers McCaslin, and the evil which permeates this history is rooted in him. His wife is never mentioned. He has a daughter by a Negro slave. He then seduces his daughter, who later gives birth to a son, Tomey's Terrel. As a result, Eunice, his first Negro mistress, drowns herself. The comment in the McCaslin ledger reads, "23 Jun 1833 Who in hell ever heard of a niger drownding him self."[25] These events prove to be sufficient to provide Ike with a sense of guilt because of his relationship to the McCaslins. Not only does he protest his own history, but he moves in his comments to the larger issue of the whole South. His family past is a paradigm of white-black relations in America.

Ike alone, of all his family, recapitulates, evaluates, and finally rejects his heritage. He does this for two reasons which in a way are inseparable. He denies that the land is his to accept, since it had never been anybody's to own and bequeath to anybody else; then, again, he refuses to accept the family

[25] *Go Down, Moses*, 267.

61

land because he wants to avoid any taint that will come with association with his past. Ownership of the land led to ownership of people. The land and people belong only to God. Absence of humility leads inevitably to lack of a moral sense. There is no end to the evil which results from a belief in strength as a justification for right. It is in this way that Ike decides to absolve himself, to reject his land and retain his integrity. It would appear to be a noble decision, but I should like to examine more closely the reasoning involved. By Ike's own assertion the land belonged solely to God:

> He made the earth first and peopled it with dumb creatures, and then He created man to be His overseer on the earth and to hold suzerainty over the earth and the animals on it in His name, not to hold for himself and his descendants inviolable title forever, generation after generation, to the oblongs and squares of the earth, but to hold the earth mutual and intact in the communal anonymity of brotherhood, and all the fee He asked was pity and humility and sufferance and endurance and the sweat of his face for bread.[26]

Man, then, was merely a tenant, but clearly a vital part of the system. The ownership of the land, the sense of "mine" that is shown as persisting and which comes full circle at the conclusion of "The Bear," leads unavoidably to a moral chaos, evil pride, disrespect for God, and most viciously to disregard for man. But man must stay in the position of responsibility in which God has placed him, particularly if he has the objective awareness of Ike. Ike comes to an awareness of evil and repudiates the land; he refuses his responsibility.

The critic who would complain about Ike's decisions or who would represent Ike as an object of Faulkner's criticism is in a lonely and unusual position, and perhaps my subsequent

[26] *Ibid.*, 257.

discussion requires some defense. Ike is presented so compassionately, with so much understanding and as so thoroughly a troubled, moral, self-examining man that it is easy to view him as heroic, even tragic. He is usually seen as a good man in an evil world, as one whose goodness is without effect because the sinners all around him have not, as it were, ears with which to hear. But Ike's repudiation of the land is no more possible than the ownership of it, by his own argument. As the Negro girl visiting him in his camp says later, Ike's repudiation of the land amounts to giving it away to someone who had even less claim to it. The past cannot be eliminated merely by turning away from it. As Faulkner clearly indicates in *Absalom, Absalom!* the past must be borne, like a burden, and understood and then absorbed and made the basis for wiser action in the present.

Ike is perhaps a much more subtle rendering of Gail Hightower or Horace Benbow. They, too, are good weak men who are made ineffectual by their "goodness." Ike is faced with the moral dilemma of a man forced to choose between his own purity of motive and the possible corruption of that motive in the service of some greater good. Ike is more like Pontius Pilate than like Christ. His ineffectuality is pathetic, not tragic, and the persistent reference to his lack of a posterity is to symbolize his isolation. When Faulkner wanted to create heroes who fight evil, he did so, as we shall see. It is the tiny, often apparently futile gestures of creatures like the little dog in "The Bear" or of the children in *Intruder* and *The Reivers* that Faulkner celebrates. Quentin commits suicide because he can see no way to come to terms with human failing. Ike gives up the land because to accept it is to consolidate the errors of the past and, incidentally, to stain his hands, as he reasons. But surely this is not a point of view which the vigorous humanistic Faulkner offers here as his own.

The critical confusion which this question evokes is an interesting illustration of what happens when Faulkner has his characters engage in philosophical debate. Faulkner is not a philosopher, and he misrepresents himself in his sententious passages. The best and clearest view of Faulkner's attitude is seen in the very spirit of his work, in the impression that the work makes. The discussion in "The Bear" necessarily leads critics into a discussion on similar lines, and they are quite likely to finish up astray. They are forced to treat Faulkner as a metaphysician at such times, and their dialectic is quite likely to be superior to his. What Ike says may in fact be "true," but what does such truth mean? Ike's skill in logic is not much help to a real world which is fallen and which is engaged in a struggle with inherited evils. We cannot all wash our hands and stand aside sadly watching evil, like Mr. Compson, even if it is only for a little while, and Faulkner most emphatically believed that we should not.

Sophonisba, daughter to Tomey's Terrel, marries an Arkansas Negro, who was brought up in the North and is educated and owns property. He takes her away to where she is later found by Ike living in near-poverty and under the threat of physical insecurity and hardship. He remonstrates with the husband and receives for argument that the hardship is compensated for by the abstract "freedom." Ike pleads with Fonsiba, but she says, "I am free." Ike, when repudiating the land uses the same words, "I am free." Now the Fonsiba episode occurs later in time than the final Ike repudiation, but earlier in the order of presentation in the novel. What is Faulkner's purpose, one is forced to ask, in inserting, rather crudely, this incident prior to its happening in time? It seems that it does, as it is intended to do, make effective comment on the abstract and futile nature of Ike's claim to freedom. One asks of Ike, as he asks of the Negro, "Freedom from what:

From work?"[27] Ike is clearly in the right in his lengthy statements criticizing the failure of the whites in their Southern role. But I am trying to demonstrate Faulkner's rejection of Ike's answer to the problem that he has defined.

Ike appears to be successfully justifying his refusal to accept his heritage until McCaslin, forsaking his dialectic, resorts to a personal comment on Ike. When the latter says that he will, by his freedom, stem the tide, or at least provide a momentary break in the course of evil, McCaslin says:

> "Chosen, I suppose (I will concede it) out of all your time by Him as you say Buck and Buddy were from theirs. And it took him a bear and an old man and four years just for you. And it took you fourteen years to reach that point and about that many, maybe more, for Old Ben, and more than seventy for Sam Fathers. And you are just one. How long then? How long?" and he [Ike]
>
> "It will be long. I have never said otherwise. But it will be all right because they will endure."[28]

But the elder cousin adds, with telling cynicism, "And anyway, you will be free."[29] It is almost startling that no one has commented on this caustic remark, the tone of which can easily be justified. Faulkner himself indicates the skepticism with which one should view Ike's abdication:

> . . . because they will endure. They will outlast us because they are—it was not a pause, barely a falter even, possibly appreciable only to himself, as if he couldn't speak even to McCaslin, even to explain his repudiation, *that which to him too, even in the act of escaping* (and maybe this was the reality and the truth of his need to escape) *was heresy*: so that even in escaping he was taking with him more of that evil and unregenerate old man who

27 *Ibid.*, 297.
28 *Ibid.*, 299.
29 *Ibid.*, 299.

could summon, because she was his property, a human being because she was old enough and female, to his widower's house and get a child on her and then dismiss her because she was of an inferior race, and then bequeath a thousand dollars to the infant, because he would be dead then and wouldn't have to pay it, than even he had feared.[30]

The use of the word "escape" cannot be casually passed by without note. Ike is afraid of the evil he has discovered, afraid of himself, unsure of the strength of his values when placed in competition with his weaknesses. Faulkner seems to want to suggest that to a great extent Ike's position is a rationalized one. For the truth is that Ike is weak.

The events following his decision further reveal his weakness. Ironically, he buys a set of tools with which to become a carpenter, simply because if they were good enough for Christ, they will be good enough for Isaac McCaslin. The latter, however, bears almost no resemblance to Christ. To begin with, Christ gave up his woodworking tools to undertake work with men, while Ike gives up men in order to become a carpenter. Christ gave up the wilderness for the city, while Ike gives up the plantation and adheres to the wilderness. Ike takes on a partner who has a daughter whom he marries. Ike loves the girl, and she has set herself the goal of forcing him to take up his rejected inheritance. If she can prevent it, she has no intention of remaining a "poor white." And so she uses sex, her only weapon, as a means of controlling Ike. She has never let him see her naked, though he has pleaded, and he on his part has remained firm in his rejection of her request that he should reassert his rights to the land. One night she undresses and before yielding to him asks again about the farm. He vehemently, too vehemently, refuses: "No, I tell you. I wont. I cant. Never"; and then later

30 *Ibid.*, 294.

this: " 'I cant. Not ever. Remember': and still the steady and invincible hand and he said Yes and he thought, *She is lost. She was born lost. We were all born lost.*"[31] Ike is weak. The significance of what follows her subsequent yielding could easily be overestimated, but Faulkner does not include it for nothing. She says: "And that's all. That's all from me. If this dont get you that son you talk about, it wont be mine."[32] Ike remains childless!

If Ike, when he rejects the land, is the Christ-like hero that R. W. B. Lewis claims he is, he must be a fallen hero in this marriage scene when he relinquishes his integrity, a scene which Lewis ignores.[33] Ike is a rather pathetic figure throughout; although he learns values and can recognize evil when he sees it, he is really unable to cope with the responsibility that ensues from such a recognition. Frequently his childlessness is emphasized by Faulkner, and this is surely to underline his separateness from the human community and his removal from the course of human destiny. This is the first sentence from *Go Down, Moses*: "Isaac McCaslin, 'Uncle Ike,' past seventy and nearer eighty than he ever corroborated any more, a widower now and uncle to half a county and father to no one."[34] In "The Bear" we find this:

> And Isaac McCaslin, not yet Uncle Ike, a long time yet before he would be uncle to half a county and still father to none, living in one small cramped fireless rented room in a Jefferson boarding-house where petit juries were domiciled during court terms and itinerant horse-and-mule-traders stayed, with his kit of brand-new carpenter's tools and the shotgun McCaslin had given him with his name engraved in silver and old General Compson's

[31] *Ibid.*, 314.
[32] *Ibid.*, 315.
[33] "Hero in the New World: William Faulkner's 'The Bear,'" *Kenyon Review*, Vol. XIII (Autumn, 1951), 641–60.
[34] *Go Down, Moses*, 3.

compass (and, when the General died, his silvermounted horn too) and the iron cot and mattress and the blankets which he would take each fall into the woods for more than sixty years and the bright tin coffee-pot.[35]

In "Delta Autumn," however, we find the clearest picture of the results of Ike's past actions. Faulkner did not tell the truth when he said in "The Bear" that Ike was returning to the woods for "one more time," because in "Delta Autumn" we are told that he has been going back every November for more than fifty years. These visits are not particularly happy ones for Ike, for they serve to remind him of the way it once was in the wilderness. Now one has to travel two hundred miles to reach it, and now the spirit of dedication to it has gone. Whereas Ike once learned basic values in the wilderness, which could be used in his dealings with men, "Delta Autumn" offers us a picture of human sin and weakness with those very woods as setting. As we shall see shortly at least one character, directly involved, attributes this state of affairs uncompromisingly to Ike.

Among the young men who now hunt with the old man is Cass's grandson, Roth Edmonds. Ike wakes one morning in the woods, to be confronted by the Negro girl whom Roth has seduced. She brings her child with her. Roth leaves money for her with Ike, while he goes hunting. Money must be her only recompense; she cannot even have the satisfaction of a personal good-bye, for Roth, in true McCaslin fashion, refuses to grant her the courtesies due to a human being. In the course of her conversation with Ike the girl makes the most precise summary analysis of Ike's failure that can be found. It comes closest, it seems to me, to an objective or a Faulkner point of view.

[35] *Ibid.*, 300.

She regarded him, almost peacefully, with that unwinking and heatless fixity—the dark wide bottomless eyes in the face's dead and toneless pallor which to the old man looked anything but dead, but young and incredibly and even ineradicably alive—as though she were not only not looking at anything, she was not even speaking to anyone but herself. "I would have made a man of him. He's not a man yet. You spoiled him. You, and Uncle Lucas and Aunt Mollie. But mostly you."

"Me?" he said. "Me?"

"Yes. When you gave to his grandfather that land which didn't belong to him, not even half of it by will or even law."[36]

Ike refuses to discuss the matter. But his silence does not invalidate her accusation that he has handed over man's future to the evil course which he had claimed to want to stop. All of Ike's arguments about the land are right, and for that very reason he is surely its most desirable "overseer."

Ike has told his camp that it is wrong to shoot does because deer are becoming more scarce. The story ends with Ike's realization that the first kill of the morning is a doe, shot by Roth. It must be remembered that Ike is weak, not evil. It should also be remembered, however, that elsewhere in Faulkner's work the good and useful figures are quite unconsciously Christ-like (the corporal, Byron Bunch, Dilsey, Chick Mallison), and it is difficult not to see as compassionate irony Faulkner's presentation of Ike withdrawing with his "brand new carpenter's tools."

As uncle to a whole county he is ineffective. He is "father to none," and the hopelessness of the evil that persists in Roth is symbolized by the fact that Roth's child is male. There will apparently be no end to the rot. Ike's only solution for the Negro girl is this one:

"Yes," he said, harshly, rapidly, but not so harsh now and soon not harsh at all but just rapid, urgent, until he knew that

36 *Ibid.*, 359–60.

his voice was running away with him and he had neither intended it nor could stop it: "That's right. Go back North. Marry:
a man in your own race. That's the only salvation for you—for a
while yet, may be a long while yet. We will have to wait. Marry
a black man. You are young, handsome, almost white; you could
find a black man who would see in you what it was you saw in
him, who would ask nothing of you and expect less and get even
still less than that, if it's revenge you want. Then you will forget
all this, forget it ever happened, that he ever existed—" until he
could stop it at last and did, sitting there in his huddle of blankets
during the instant when, without moving at all, she blazed
silently down at him. Then that was gone too. She stood in the
gleaming and still dripping slicker, looking quietly down at him
from under the sodden hat.

"Old man," she said, "have you lived so long and forgotten
so much that you dont remember anything you ever knew or
felt or even heard about love?"[37]

Christ never gave such unsatisfactory answers to either his
followers or his accusers as Ike gives here. Love does not wait
on time; man, not fate, must shape history.

It would seem that a pathetic figure has been mistaken by
the critics for a sympathetic one. Ike represents Faulkner's
point of view only in occasional sentences. The course which
Ike follows in the novel is so drawn as to clearly indicate
Faulkner's rejection of it. The course he should have followed
is discoverable if one traces back the arguments of Ike and
his cousin. There he reveals an awareness that he later betrays; he refuses to hold the land as God's overseer, even
though he knows that this is required; he forsakes all obligation.

Ike was the first, and as far as we know, the only member
of his family with moral awareness. Only he had Sam Fathers
for father, who taught him the values which McCaslin, his

[37] *Ibid.*, 363.

cousin, reiterated: *"Courage and honor and pride, and pity and love of justice and of liberty. They all touch the heart, and what the heart holds to becomes truth, as far as we know truth."*[38] Yet Ike, despite his moral equipment, remains socially ineffectual. He is unable to take part in human affairs, unable to do as Dilsey does in *The Sound and the Fury* or as the corporal does in *A Fable*, to apply his values to his circumstances, to operate in the real world with the knowledge of his heart. The shock of the discovery of evil led to what Faulkner himself calls escape. But Ike cannot escape, for as we see in "Delta Autumn," in Aristotelian fashion, evil always comes home to roost, even when the evil is the result of a negative rather than of a positive sin.

"The Bear" is not a successful work of fiction. It was an adequate short story when it first appeared in *Harper's*, and since then it has gained greatly in prose style and power, but it has become more confused too. Nor does this confusion arise merely from the insertion of the McCaslin family history, though this does hinder the unity of an otherwise connected story—the aesthetic unity, that is, not the technical one. The heart of the matter is that although the subject, the thesis, is the same here as in the rest of Faulkner's fiction, this *novella* suffers from the imposition of a point of view on the fictional content. Here again, though not so blatantly as in *A Fable*, a novel has been constructed so as to bring forth an idea, almost an ideology, with a disregard for the demand of fiction that it be true to itself.

Sylvan Schendler, in his study of *A Fable*, makes this comment:

> Recently, Faulkner has given evidence that he has accepted the role of "engaged" writer whose responsibility it is to offer solu-

[38] *Ibid.*, 297.

71

tions to, or at least to respond to, the urgent moral problems of our time. In his approach to these problems, Faulkner apparently feels it necessary to make his views explicit apart from whatever form they may be given in the creative unity of his work.[39]

As I hope to show, Faulkner was always the "engaged writer," but that he has become explicit in the last group of novels is indisputable. I do not mean that his point of view has emerged more clearly—in some ways the new technique makes it less precise, since imagination imposes its own unity on an artist's work. I mean, rather, that the didactic and philosophic intention has been given license to intrude, in almost any way it chooses, to the corruption of artistic integrity.

One can demonstrate the damage done by this method by showing specific inconsistencies in the hunting section of "The Bear." Symbol here does not grow out of the figures in the story; it is imposed upon them, in a contrived way, as the hawk is imposed on the living room in Glenway Wescott's story.[40] For instance, at one point, Ike and Sam go to meet the bear:

> Timing them as if they were meeting an appointment with another human being, himself carrying the fyce with a sack over its head and Sam Fathers with a brace of the hounds on a rope leash, they lay downwind of the trail and actually ambushed the bear. They were so close that it turned at bay although he realised later this might have been from surprise and amazement at the shrill and frantic uproar of the fyce. It turned at bay against the trunk of a big cypress, on its hind feet.[41]

[39] "William Faulkner's A Fable" (unpublished dissertation, Northwestern University, 1956), 196.

[40] Glenway Wescott's story, "The Pilgrim Hawk," seems to me to contain a perfect modern illustration of a highly contrived and artificial symbol that detracts rather than adds to the realism of the story.

[41] Go Down, Moses, 211.

72

After this incident Sam says to the boy:

> "You've done seed him twice now, with a gun in your hands,"
> he said. "This time you couldn't have missed him."
> The boy rose. He still held the fyce. Even in his arms it con-
> tinued to yap frantically, surging and straining toward the fading
> sound of the hounds like a collection of live-wire springs. The
> boy was panting a little. "Neither could you," he said. "You had
> the gun. Why didn't you shoot him?"
> Sam didn't seem to have heard.[42]

It is very convenient of Sam not to hear, since of course, in
terms of the story, there is no answer. Sam is a hunter, and this
is a bear which they have been trying for years to kill. Sam or
the boy is obliged to shoot him, yet when the opportunity
arises, they refuse. Let us momentarily concede that this is
acceptable, that neither felt it was fair to kill the bear in ambush,[43] even making such a concession for that episode, how
can one possibly justify Sam's peculiar insistence that it is
impossible to catch the bear without the right dog, when we
are explicitly told how easy it was to ambush him: "Too big.
We aint got the dog yet. But maybe some day."[44] I am trying
to explain the impossibilities of the story on the narrative
level. If the dog Lion is to be anything more than a symbol, he
must not only be absolutely necessary to the hunt, which as
we see he is not, but he must also be more like a real dog and
less like Thurber's lawn dog.

It is impossible to explain Boon's visit to Memphis, except
as part of the symbolic structure. Boon, as the figure I have
described earlier, is more fully explained by his conduct in
Memphis, but on what grounds does this isolated incident,

[42] *Ibid.*, 212.

[43] It is apparently fair, however, to lie in wait for a doe at her bedding
place and shoot her as she returns, as Ike does.

[44] *Go Down, Moses*, 24.

73

actually a story in itself, have a place in the hunting narrative? It breaks the rhythm and suspense and destroys the continuity of the wilderness setting. These are all faults in structure and consistency. When we turn to the discussion between Ike and Cass, we find further reason for critical concern, for here is the sententious debate, here all the preaching and philosophy, not embodied in and arising out of the essence of the fiction. The debate is brilliantly written and convincing in itself, but it is structually obtrusive. It is Faulkner's debate with himself. There is little reason to attack it as a breach of unity, since it merely extends in a forthright and literal way the symbolic nature of the rest, yet it clearly wrenches into the human arena, in a needlessly violent way, the lessons learned in the wilderness. Moreover, it cuts the ground away from under the hunting story and makes foolish its pretense to be anything but symbolic juggling. We have writing here that veers toward allegory because the symbols do not suggest implications arising out of their very nature. Meanings are imposed by the author's intention. "The Bear" fails from its contrived nature. Its metaphors are not constructed out of the observable world of Faulkner's experience but are welded together artificially from Faulkner's intellect. The story is meaningless unless we understand the intended significance of the author's characters and events. Sam's death, for instance, is not explained away by the doctor's lecture on the power of mind over matter.

The critics can come to little agreement on the roles of Boon and Sam, and the bear itself has been called many things. But all critics are agreed that Faulkner had in mind a set of equivalents that are almost, if not quite, specific. Fiction must embody its point of view in a reality produced by the imagination. It is through the use of metaphor, image, and epithet that literature comes alive. The writer at his best

74

sees his picture clearly, then makes us see what he sees, no less in prose than in poetry. Faulkner has let his point of view emerge here, not clearly, but sufficiently in his own mind to damage his attempt to write satisfactory fiction. He has again resorted to what we might call the explicit method of fiction. R. W. B. Lewis, with characteristic restraint, puts it this way: "Faulkner himself is most willing, too willing perhaps, that we should recognize the universal design into which his southern saga fits; he plants, if anything, too many clues to his wider ranges of meaning."[45] The "wider ranges of meaning" should be a result of the writer's having written movingly of the world as he sees it. When a "message" is the impulse, the fiction drags limply after.

[45] "Hero in the New World: William Faulkner's 'The Bear,'" *Kenyon Review*, Vol. XIII (Autumn, 1951), 656.

CHAPTER IV

Intruder in the Dust
"There is always somewhere someone"

I*ntruder in the Dust* pretends to be a novel in the murder-mystery genre. As in the case of the other later novels, the thin narrative veneer fails to obscure the all too obvious fact that the developing consciousness of the characters and a play with philosophical abstractions are the central concern. In this case the attempt to write for all levels of perception and appreciation leads to failure all around. There are three distinct "areas" of treatment: the purely narrative, the race-relations theme, and, arising out of the latter, the humanistic theme. This last concern is the primary motivating one of the novel. It was conceived first and then dressed in a contrived plot. However, writing of a geographical area that he knows best, where the emotional climate is tense with the over-whelming problem of race relations, Faulkner finds himself unable to avoid social commentary and the explicit presentation of a point of view. The confusion which results from this chaos of purpose once again demonstrates how Faulkner's work has suffered from his willingness to forego the dictates of his imagination in favor of the urgency of his rationale.

The plot is relatively simple. Lucas Beauchamp, an aging Negro, is partially descended from white McCaslins; because of his origin and because of his natural qualities, he has a dignity which irks everybody and earns him the hatred of the white community—he refuses to "be a nigger first." Lucas makes the acquaintance of the white boy, Charles (Chick) Mallison, when the latter is twelve years old. The circumstances of this meeting are central to the novel, because at their meeting, the Negro renders the white boy a service which the boy spends four years trying hopelessly to repay. At last, however, the boy believes that Lucas has forgotten him entirely, absolved him of his debt. Four years elapse, and the relationship seems to have sunk into oblivion, when Lucas is suddenly arrested on suspicion, or more accurately on the "certainty," of his having committed murder. When he is brought to the jail, he notices Chick in the crowd and tells him to bring his uncle, Gavin Stevens, the lawyer. Lucas refuses to talk about his guilt or innocence to Stevens unless the latter will commit himself to taking the case. Gavin is likewise stubborn and will not take the case unless Lucas explains all the circumstances. Gavin is, therefore, rejected and Lucas protests his innocence to Chick, explaining that the bullet in the dead man is not from his gun. Chick, driven by motives we will discuss later, undertakes to dig up the grave of the murdered man with the help of his young Negro friend and an old lady. After many technicalities the innocence of Lucas is established, thus corroborating what was for the reader a foregone conclusion.

This is the skeleton of the plot, but since Faulkner is more interested here in other elements, the plot often suffers from unreasonable compressions, omissions, and illogicalities. In order to arrive at the intended meaning of the novel, we must look more closely at the events summarized above. It is important here to emphasize certain characteristics, common to Faulkner's fiction, which bear on this novel and throw light on its meaning. Childishness and maturity are never automatically correlative with age in Faulkner's work. A young boy, like the ten year old Isaac McCaslin of "The Bear," can be more mature in moral terms than almost all the adults around him. Boon Hogganbeck, for instance, in the same novel, is a man with the mind of a child. Benjy in *The Sound and the Fury* is thirty-three years of age with the mind of an infant, while the child who tells the short story "Uncle Willy" is the only person therein who is able to recognize a saint when one appears. There are numerous examples of Faulkner's rejection of the popular cliché that age equals wisdom.

Faulkner's concern with children and the child's point of view is derived from his awareness of the effect of the past on the present, not only in the general way in which the past bequeathes its established institutions, but in the specific teachings and beliefs handed down directly from generation to generation. In this way each generation possesses the faults and qualities of its forebears. As Gavin Stevens says, "No man can cause more grief than that one clinging blindly to the vices of his ancestors."[1] In this way the child, not yet fully conditioned by usage and acquaintance, assumes a special significance in Faulkner's work, because the child, being newer and less rigid, is capable of the greater sympathy and more ready willingness to judge each individual as an individual. Benjy Compson, the child Snopes of "Barn Burning," Isaac McCaslin, the young Bayard Sartoris of *The Unvanquished*, and the idiot in *Sanctuary* are able to see with clearer, more innocent eyes, and to judge by more human and less abstract standards. In his essay on *Huckleberry Finn*, Lionel Trilling makes this astute comment:

> No one, as he [Twain] well knew, sets a higher value on truth than a boy. Truth is the whole of a boy's conscious demand upon the world of adults. He is likely to believe that the adult world is in a conspiracy to lie to him, and it is this belief, by no means unfounded, that arouses Tom and Huck and all boys to their moral sensitivity, their everlasting concern with justice, which they call fairness. At the same time it often makes them skillful

[1] William Faulkner, *Intruder in the Dust* (New York, 1948), 49.

and profound liars in their own defense, yet they do not tell the
ultimate lie of adults: they do not lie to themselves.[2]

It is this refusal to lie to itself, this ability to face reality and
answer problems in "fair" or humanistic terms, that for Faulkner characterizes the mature mind. Thus in Faulkner's work
the young person when shown sympathetically (and he
usually is) comes to symbolize the ideal, or at least promising,
human being, and is designed to represent a moral outlook to
inspire the reader. The clues to Faulkner's point of view are
often to be found in his simple-minded characters.

With these facts in mind, we may more fully appreciate
Chick Mallison's role in *Intruder in the Dust*. There is probably no design on Faulkner's part in his having chosen the
name Chick, and yet even a passing acquaintance with his
work soon suggests that his names usually are selected with
great care: Benjamin, Vardaman, Jewel, Sartoris, Temple, and
Joe Christmas give a representative indication of this nominal
significance. Chick's name may or may not be intentionally
significant. While it is a common nickname for Charles, Faulkner is not compelled to use it. Surely he symbolizes, as his
name suggests, the innocent human being, who has not yet
suffered the loss of spontaneity and human sympathy, as have
those around him who dedicate themselves to the further
divisiveness of a competitive materialism. The shopkeepers
do not even have time to be ashamed: "They couldn't shut
up the stores and run home too yet; there still might be a
chance to sell each other a nickel's worth of something."[3]

Early in the novel a conflict takes place in Chick between
the ingrained prejudices and views of his environment and
tradition and his natural tendency towards fairness and truth.

[2] *The Liberal Imagination* (New York, 1950), 104.
[3] *Intruder in the Dust*, 203.

That he has the integrity, the individuality, to be the field for such a conflict makes him "unique" among his neighbors:

> . . . the dirt, the earth which had bred his bones and those of his fathers for six generations . . . was still shaping him into not just a man but a specific man, not with just a man's passions and aspirations and beliefs but the specific passions and hopes and convictions and ways of thinking and acting of a specific kind and even race: and even more: even among a kind and race specific and unique (according to the lights of most, certainly of all of them who had thronged into town this morning to stand across the street from the jail and crowd up around the sheriff's car, damned unique).[4]

Following this line of reasoning, one might say that every child is, in the beginning, unique.

Before the conflict is presented, we see the other, growing side of Chick's character as the ordinary, "the average" Southern white boy with the "right" middle-class views. One winter day he is invited to shoot rabbits on the Edmonds' estate. He falls into a creek. Trying to get out, the boy finds that Lucas has arrived and is standing on the bank, staring at him. He "had made no effort whatever to help him up out of the creek, had in fact ordered Aleck Sander [Chick's Negro friend] to desist with the pole which had been the one token toward help that anybody had made."[5] The incident is, of course, symbolic, since besides providing the opportunity for Chick to meet Lucas, it also characterizes their relationship. Lucas does force Chick at this point to help himself. In fact, Lucas says that any help given him would be a hindrance: "Get the pole out of his way so he can get out."[6]

Having established their basic relationship, Lucas as the

[4] *Ibid.*, 151.
[5] *Ibid.*, 6.
[6] *Ibid.*, 6.

savior of Chick, Faulkner proceeds to sketch it in more fully. Lucas guides Chick away from the creek to the Negro cabin where he lives. Chick makes a feeble protest against going but finally yields, and while walking there, he tries to rationalize his action:

> . . . he knew that the true reason was that he could no more imagine himself contradicting the man striding on ahead of him than he could his grandfather, not from any fear of nor even the threat of reprisal but because like his grandfather the man striding ahead of him was simply incapable of conceiving himself by a child contradicted and defied.[7]

At this point Chick is a child not only in years but in moral stature too. He has not yet begun the struggle between his instincts and the imposed local code. Lucas is the man, the leader, the mature guide. He is above all concerned with truth in human relationships; this preoccupation later lands him, falsely accused, in jail. It is his interference in somebody else's business, out of a sense of justice and human involvement, that ironically enough leads to his persecution. And his rejection of material values is clearly symbolized at the end of the novel, after he pays Stevens:

> [He] . . . snapped the purse shut and put it back inside his coat and with the other hand shoved the whole mass of coins and the crumpled bill across the table until the desk blotter stopped them and took a bandana handkerchief from the side pocket of the coat and wiped his hands and put the handkerchief back and stood again intractable and calm.[8]

This maturity is illustrated earlier by what follows when he and Chick arrive in his cabin.

Chick is given dinner, which he later realizes "had been not

[7] *Ibid.*, 8.
[8] *Ibid.*, 247.

81

just the best Lucas had to offer but all he had to offer."[9] Lucas gives "all he had to offer," not with a view to reward or because he is playing the traditional role of the subservient Negro, but because, being Lucas, he could not do otherwise. After the dinner comes the incident which is central to the novel. The boy tries to pay for the meal:

> [He] . . . extended the coins: and in the same second in which he knew she would have taken them he knew that only by that one irrevocable second was he forever now too late, forever beyond recall, standing with the slow hot blood as slow as minutes themselves up his neck and face, forever with his dumb hand open and on it the four shameful fragments of milled and minted dross, until at last the man had something that at least did the office of pity.
>
> "What's that for?" the man said, not even moving, not even tilting his face downward to look at what was on his palm: for another eternity and only the hot dead moveless blood until at last it ran to rage so that at least he could bear the shame: and watched his palm turn over not flinging the coins but spurning them downward ringing onto the bare floor, bouncing and one of the nickels even rolling away in a long swooping curve with a dry minute sound like the scurry of a small mouse.[10]

But Lucas is above and beyond even insult; his pride in his manhood is so surely fixed that he is imperturbable, and his parting remark is a good-natured one: " 'Now go on and shoot your rabbit,' the voice said. 'And stay out of that creek.' "[11]

One meaning of this incident is best illustrated by reference to a similar event in the story "The Fire and the Hearth." At a time much earlier than that of the events of *Intruder*, Edmonds, as a boy, is accustomed, out of close friendship, to sleep in the same bed with a Negro boy, Henry, son of Lucas

[9] *Ibid.*, 17.
[10] *Ibid.*, 15–16.
[11] *Ibid.*, 16.

Beauchamp and Molly. One night Edmonds insists that Henry sleep on the floor. Henry agrees and rests quietly.

> But the boy didn't sleep, long after Henry's quiet and untroubled breathing had begun, lying in a rigid fury of the grief he could not explain, the shame he would not admit. Then he slept and it seemed to him he was still awake, waked and did not know he had slept until he saw in the gray of dawn the empty pallet on the floor. They did not hunt that morning. They never slept in the same room again and never again ate at the same table because he admitted to himself it was shame now . . . . Then one day he knew it was grief and was ready to admit it was shame also, wanted to admit it only it was too late then, forever and forever too late.[12]

He tries to go back to the previous relationship, but there is no going back. When he goes to eat with the Negro family, he finds that they have accepted his self-created barriers, and they set his place alone at the table. " 'Are you ashamed to eat when I eat?' he cried. Henry paused, turning his head a little to speak in the voice slow and without heat: 'I aint shamed of nobody,' he said peacefully. 'Not even me.' So he entered his heritage. He ate its bitter fruit."[13]

The "bitter fruit," then, is a major concern in the Faulkner canon. The white man engenders an inhuman or even nonhuman separation between people, by insisting on the validity of abstractions that grow out of the past, rather than reacting to people out of his own best instincts and regarding each individual in his own right in the present. People do not let themselves like other people even when they want to.

Chick Mallison's insult to Lucas is a symbolic drama treating of Negro-white relations. The white boy "lowers" himself and shows himself inferior in the very act of demonstrating

[12] *Go Down, Moses*, 112.
[13] *Ibid.*, 113–14.

his superiority. Environment has compelled Chick to act as he does, to insult his fellow man, but the fact that he can be horribly shamed, the fact of his own awareness, indicates his natural tendency towards fellow-feeling and kindness. To offer money was not Chick's idea, but the voice of his society speaking through him. Through his shame the boy comes to question his own attitude and the values of the society around him. At first he rationalizes his torment of shame into a need to pay the debt to Lucas. In reality it is a debt to himself that he must pay. Lucas is aware of no debt. The boy must free his own instinctive humanity and thus invalidate the imaginary obligation. He must make his stature commensurate with Lucas'. He, too, must be a man. First, however, he tries to put himself in the right. In order to justify his own smallness, he finds himself "writhing with impotent fury" and thinking what "every white man in that whole section of the country had been thinking about him for years: *We got to make him be a nigger first. He's got to admit he's a nigger.*"[14] But he is one of those who "protest too much." His real solution must ultimately be found, not by forcing anything on Lucas, but by examining himself. This understanding of the first chapter is vital to an accurate understanding of the symbolic meaning of the rest of the novel.

Four years after these events, Lucas is arrested for murder. The boy pretends to himself that he feels great relief: "Because he was free. Lucas was no longer his responsibility, he was no longer Lucas' keeper; Lucas himself had discharged him."[15] But it turns out that Lucas has not discharged him from the obligation to moral growth. Lucas has not lowered himself into the inferior position that would justify Chick's insulting him and thus free the boy from shame. Lucas is in-

14 *Intruder in the Dust*, 18.
15 *Ibid.*, 42.

nocent, and it falls to the lot of Chick Mallison to prove Lucas'
innocence, and thereby at the same time to establish his own
moral integrity. If he can pursue the course of truth, he will
have, not eradicated, but at least invalidated the past, and
have proved his own capacity for self-reliance as a man, and
symbolically, as a race.

When Lucas sends for Gavin Stevens, he does so in order to
make a formal contract with a defense attorney. We must
always remember that although Faulkner is not really interested in writing a "pot-boiler," he finds himself unwillingly
compelled to sustain a believable narrative. The failure of
Stevens to believe Lucas, to take the case on trust, is necessary
to make Lucas' dependence on Chick a real one, growing out
of need. It is also for symbolic purposes, however, that Chick
is the person who must help Lucas.

On a slight pretext Chick is able to visit Lucas alone, after
Stevens has left without establishing any effective communication with the Negro. In fact, Stevens is shown in his interview to be still bound by considerations of class, even though
the Negro's life is under immediate threat. " 'Lucas,' he said,
'has it ever occurred to you that if you just said mister to white
people and said it like you meant it, you might not be sitting
here now?' "[16] The boy, on the other hand, is shown, on leaving
the jail, to be torn by the conflict between his enculturated
prejudices and his natural curiosity for truth: *"thinking a
nigger a murderer who shoots white people in the back and
aint even sorry.* He said: 'I imagine I'll find Skeets McGowan
loafing somewhere on the Square. He's got a key to the drug-

---

[16] *Ibid.*, 62. This is, ironically enough, true, since Lucas would not be the
kind of person in that case who would risk his life in the cause of fairness.
Faulkner is satirizing his society with this ironic statement which suggests
that it is the noble, upright, and principled human beings who find themselves the victims of an outraged society.

store. I'll take Lucas some tobacco tonight.' His uncle stopped."[17]

On his return to the jail, Chick immediately asks what is required of him, like the sinner seeking instructions for his penance from the priest. He says to Lucas, "All right. What do you want me to do?"[18] Lucas requires him to go and look at the dead body. The boy asks why: " 'All right,' he said. 'Then what?' 'He wasn't shot with no fawty-one Colt.' 'What was he shot with?' But Lucas didn't answer that."[19]

At this point only a symbolic interpretation makes the story meaningful. Lucas is here treating the boy as he did at the creek, four years earlier. He is requiring Chick to act in his own interest, to seek for truth, to assess his own situation. It is certain that Lucas, who seems almost indifferent to death and refuses to relate in detail the incident of the murder, does not require Chick to act in his behalf.

> . . . because Lucas was not even asking him to believe anything; he was not even asking a favor, making no last desperate plea to his humanity and pity but was even going to pay him provided the price was not too high, to go alone seventeen miles (no, nine: he remembered at least that he had heard that now) in the dark and risk being caught violating the grave of a member of a clan of men already at the pitch to commit the absolute of furious and bloody outrage, without even telling him why.[20]

In his search for innocence it becomes quite clear to Chick that he cannot expect help even from the person with whom

[17] *Ibid.*, 66. Irving Howe, in his *William Faulkner: A Critical Study*, has pointed out the similarity between this conflict and that which takes place in Huck Finn. In both cases there is the split allegiance, on the one hand to the values of the white society, and on the other to the natural leanings of the heart. In both cases the boys follow the heart.

[18] *Intruder in the Dust*, 68.

[19] *Ibid.*, 69.

[20] *Ibid.*, 72.

he has established his closest relationship, Gavin, his uncle. His uncle follows the pattern of Southern white response to Lucas' plight: "... even his uncle too: 'Suppose it then. Lucas should have thought of that before he shot a white man in the back.' "[21]

There are, however, two people upon whom Chick can rely for help. One is his young Negro friend, Aleck Sander, the son of his family's servant, and the other is old Miss Habersham, the descendant of one of the oldest families in Jefferson. In order to understand the significance of their inclusion in the "mercy-group," one must analyze the meaning of what it is they have to do. Lucas we know asked Chick to go out to the churchyard and look at the body of the murdered man in order to ascertain that it was not his gun which fired the bullet that killed Vinson Gowrie. Faulkner chooses the titles of his novels with great care. He who digs up the grave is in a literal sense an intruder in the dust. But in another sense the examination of a dead body in a grave is an examination of the past. Dust is a metaphor for time; it is often used at burial services.[22] The body of man returns to the dust of which it was originally composed. In fact, the popular metaphor "to dig up the past" might usefully be recalled here. When Chick is asked to dig up a corpse, he is being asked to examine the past. On the one hand this is necessary in order that he, as representative of a race, should determine the justness of his relationship with Lucas, the white man as accuser of the black, and on the other hand it is important that Chick should find out the truth for himself rather than accept the prevailing and long-standing ideas of his society.

With the exception of the three "grave-diggers," everyone

21 *Ibid.*, 80.
22 "Burial of the Dead. At the Grave," *Book of Common Prayer* (New York, 1929), 333.

is convinced that Lucas is the murderer, and whatever he says to the contrary must be a lie. That it is a young Negro and an old woman who join in the examination of the past signifies much. The inclusion of the young Negro suggests that the two races of the South must join together in innocence and open-mindedness to determine the truth, whence they can go forward on a new footing based on a common goal and the unity of their humanity. Miss Habersham represents the best of the past; she works side by side with a Negro, selling vegetables; she had also "stood up in the Negro church as godmother to Molly's first chile."[23] She, too, must be taken along in the search for understanding. In fact, Miss Habersham is the guiding force in the search. It is she who organizes Chick's urge to help Lucas and himself. But Chick is aware that it is a sad commentary on his society, on all society, that the responsibility for truth must depend on such as Miss Habersham. "[He] thought *She's too old for this* and then corrected it: *No a woman a lady shouldn't have to do this*"[24]; and later, "*She's too old for this, to have to do this.*"[25]

The actual digging, the examination of the past, reveals the extent to which the present is living in the blind acceptance of falsehood. It turns out that the body in the grave is not that of the murdered man. This discovery leads to the realization that there are two murdered men. Symbolically, it indicates a greater evil in the past than the present wants to admit. The simple judgments and crude prejudices of society turn out to be baseless, and reason and examination lead to an understanding of the underlying complexities of an apparently obvious situation.

It appears to me unnecessary here to go into the mechanics

23 *Intruder in the Dust*, 87.
24 *Ibid.*, 112.
25 *Ibid.*, 116.

of the ensuing plot. The early events of the novel provide the whole focus, after which Faulkner is obliged to pursue elaborations that provide no new information of any importance. The innocence of Lucas, once proved, undermines the story on its narrative level by removing whatever suspense was originally present. In fact, the second half of the novel is largely taken up with the pseudophilosophical ramblings of Gavin Stevens, who as the occasional mounthpiece of Faulkner, can never quite make the distinction between a universal commentary on man and a series of observations on race relations in the South. It would seem that Faulkner, when he came to this novel, had not really found a new way, or a satisfactory way, of saying the one thing.[26] Only thus can one explain the trailing off in the novel, the self-consciousness, and the unjustifiable intrusion of sermonizing that is unrelated to the plot. The question of style thus looms large in any consideration of *Intruder*, and it is to this that we should now proceed.

As with the other novels published between 1948 and 1954, two basic faults of style become obvious in *Intruder in the Dust*. One is actually a structural fault; the other is a stylistic fault which amounts in fiction to a breach of good taste. In the first place, the failure of manner and matter to emerge as a unified conception from the author's imagination leads to a breakdown in the effort to sustain a coherent and credible narrative. Whereas in the most effective literature we find the story level and the symbolic implications sustaining each other, here the "levels" or ranges of connotation intrude upon each other. There are several instances of this. The key inci-

---

[26] At Nagano, Faulkner said: "I'm inclined to think that [all of a man's] work has such a definite relationship that he doesn't in mid-career change his stride, or his purpose. . . . it is basically directed towards the same point, and this was—I think I've spoken of this once before—it is the desire of the artist before he dies to say all he possibly can of what he knows of truth in the most moving way." *Nagano*, 46.

dent of the novel, the one which provides a basis for all that
follows, is Chick's falling into the creek on the Edmonds'
estate. Yet about this Faulkner says that "he [Chick] didn't
know how it happened,"[27] and then describes the event in
this way:

> . . . he didn't know how it happened, something a girl might
> have been expected and even excused for doing but nobody else,
> halfway over the footlog and not even thinking about it who had
> walked the top rail of a fence many a time twice that far when
> all of a sudden the known familiar sunny winter earth was up-
> side down.[28]

It seems to me that this is an example of the writer's con-
ceiving first the symbolic situation that he requires and then
finding for it a physical setting. The above description seems
designed to convince Faulkner as much as any one else. In a
similar way Lucas' refusal to communicate his innocence to
Gavin Stevens and his preference for Chick as his defendant
is not credible on the terms which Faulkner uses to explain it.
Lucas, we are told, knows by experience and intuition that
"If you ever needs to get anything done outside the common
run, dont waste yo time on the menfolks; get the womens and
children to working at it."[29] But in that case, why ask to see
Stevens in the first place? It cannot be to assert his "Negro-
hood," because his self-assurance is deep-seated; we have
already seen his total unconcern with the views of the community. He is giving Stevens as the representative of the white
men, the opportunity to free himself from the burden of guilt.
Stevens refuses and Chick takes over. Only through the symbolic explanation that Chick is the right person to ask, because

[27] *Intruder in the Dust*, 4.
[28] *Ibid.*, 5.
[29] *Ibid.*, 71–72.

he is not yet totally committed to the values of his society, can the entire episode be fully comprehended.

Betrayal of the plot reaches its extremes in the many passages where, without justification by the narrative, the characters, especially Stevens, make speeches or undergo internal reflection. The instances of this fault are too numerous to mention, and two or three examples must suffice to demonstrate their ineptness. The seventh chapter contains several consecutive pages of comment on the relationship of the South and the North and ends with the statement that together they comprise "a mass of people who no longer have anything in common save a frantic greed for money and a basic fear of a failure of national character which they hide from one another behind a loud lipservice to a flag."[30] These remarks obviously have little or nothing to do with the action of the novel.

Chapter Ten contains a political speech, more or less on the same subject, which is weakly integrated into the novel by the device of having Chick recall his uncle's aphoristic pronouncements. Here Faulkner has been forced by his urgent rationale to drop all pretense at writing fiction. The same is true of the following:

> Not all white people can endure slavery and apparently no man can stand freedom (Which incidentally—the premise that man really wants peace and freedom—is the trouble with our relations with Europe right now, whose people not only dont know what peace is but—except for Anglo Saxons—actively fear and distrust personal liberty; we are hoping without really any hope that our atom bomb will be enough to defend an idea as obsolete at Noah's Ark.); with one mutual instantaneous accord he forces his liberty into the hands of the first demagogue who rises into view: lacking that he himself destroys and obliterates it from his

[30] *Ibid.*, 156.

sight and ken and even remembrance with the frantic unanimity of a neighborhood stamping out a grass-fire. But the people named Sambo survived the one and who knows? they may even endure the other.[31]

These illustrations of failure are found in a novel by a writer who, when the imagination naturally answers his needs, can write in the same novel:

> [He] leaned first out the open window to look back then turned in the seat to see back through the rear window, watching them still in their rapid unblurred diminishment—the man and the mule and the wooden plow which coupled them furious and solitary, fixed and without progress in the earth, leaning terrifically against nothing.[32]

This surely says what needs to be said in a much more powerful and compressed way and in no measure violates the narrative. All this is not to say that when Faulkner turns pamphleteer he is not effective. But the pamphleteer and the novelist are made of different material. Although the twentieth century witnessed the disappearance of the author from the structure of the novel and fiction gained a measure of realism in consequence, Faulkner has shown that he for one cannot always restrain his ideas from becoming intrusive, however much he tries to dramatize them.

In *Intruder*, Faulkner chooses to propagandize about matters which he had earlier confined to comments outside of his fiction. Yet aside from those comments dealing with the internal politics of the United States, the main thesis of this novel is the same as that of all the other novels. It is the proposition that the only salvation for man, in or after life, lies in the emphasis on and the devotion to a humanistic existence.

[31] *Ibid.*, 149–50.
[32] *Ibid.*, 148.

Man must find and cherish those values which are fundamentally human, and for Faulkner these are personal integrity, love of fellow-man, and a faith in the fundamental goodness of all men. All men have the same emotions and needs, and Faulkner in his best work is intent on revealing them. I do not believe that Faulkner is merely being clever when he makes Gavin say about the American, "In fact he doesn't really love that bank-account nearly as much as foreigners like to think because he will spend almost any or all of it for almost anything provided it is valueless enough."[33] Nor do I believe that the word "valueless" is used here carelessly. In many novels Faulkner disparagingly portrays a valueless society, or at least a society valuing the wrong things. Value resides only in those beliefs which provide a satisfying answer to man's questions about existence and which provide a code for living which will enable the individual to retain his dignity and satisfy his inmost conscience.

Faulkner sees the need for examining one's place in a tradition, for questioning the beliefs that are handed down from one generation to another, and for the refusal to accept meaningless dogma. The responsibility of the individual to seek out truth is paramount to all other tasks, because it is part of the responsibility to eternity: "It's all now you see. Yesterday wont be over until tomorrow and tomorrow began ten thousand years ago."[34]

[33] *Ibid.*, 238–39.
[34] *Ibid.*, 194.

CHAPTER V

Requiem for a Nun
"The tragic life of a prostitute"

The similarity between *Requiem for a Nun* and *Intruder in the Dust* is striking enough to be worthy of comment. Considered together, they reflect each other's meanings and reveal mutual weaknesses. These two stand together chronologically and stylistically. Between their publication in 1951 and 1948 respectively, Faulkner published nothing of any significance. Both are murder stories in the most general sense. They are both characterized by sententious monologue, didacticism, overt moralizing, and a circuitous style. Both novels fail to present skillfully wrought or feasible plots: the plot is often summarized and always sacrificed to its presentation. It is even more significant that in both these novels a Negro makes a sacrifice in order to challenge and assist the integrity of his white neighbor; in each novel the heroic Negro is mostly seen in jail; each is forced into his predicament by the white man's wickedness; both stories are set in Jefferson. Gavin Stevens plays an important role in each case. Furthermore, we will see that a re-examination of the past is central to each novel, and that as a result of this probing, the white man gains a new measure of moral maturity.

Requiem for a Nun is really two novels, or rather, one novel and one play. To say even this is not really to describe the work accurately, because the long prose sections of *Requiem* are descriptive rather than narrative. There are, undoubtedly, two distinct parts to the work. Their connection is a tenuous one, arising from a common geographical background and

similar themes. Both deal with good and evil and the omni-
presence of the past. The juxtaposition of the two parts serves
to accentuate the themes which they treat of separately.

The "dramatic" section provides the only plot to be found in
the novel. Temple Drake, the onetime victim of a perverted
"corn cob assault" and an enforced stay in a "cat-house," has
now married the young man who was partially responsible
for her predicament. He felt obliged to become her husband,
the father of her children, as a sort of atonement. There is no
unity in the family, and when the brother of her past lover
turns up to blackmail Temple, she prepares to run away with
him. Nancy, the Negro maid, has other ideas and murders
Temple's baby to force her to stay. The novel is, for the most
part, concerned with the resultant awakening of Temple to the
real nature of her past life and with the rise of her moral
responsibility.

As in the case of the novels we have discussed so far, we
find that there is really no narrative drama and only the flimsiest of plots; the story is merely an inadequate pretext for a
Faulkner sermon. Here again the conflict between the narrative and the philosophical levels destroys both. There are in
fact no levels; all is on one plane. There is ample evidence to
show that the intended dramatic basis of the story, the fight
to save Nancy's life, is a baseless pretense. When Nancy has
already been condemned and Temple and the reader are still
under the illusion that Stevens is trying to win a reprieve, this
dialogue takes place:

TEMPLE: ". . . We're trying to save a condemned murderess
whose lawyer has already admitted that he has failed. What has
truth got to do with that?"

STEVENS: ". . . We're not concerned with death. That's nothing:
any handful of petty facts and sworn documents can cope with
that. That's all finished now; we can forget it. What we are trying

to deal with now is injustice. Only truth can cope with that. Or love."[1]

A little later a similarly enigmatic dialogue occurs:

> STEVENS: ". . . We're going to the Governor. Tonight."
> TEMPLE: "The Governor!"
> STEVENS: "Perhaps he wont save her either. He probably wont."
> TEMPLE: "Then why ask him? Why?"
> STEVENS: "I've told you. Truth."
> TEMPLE (in quiet amazement): "For no more than that. For no better reason than that. Just to get it told, breathed aloud, into words, sound. Just to be heard by, told to, someone, anyone, any stranger none of whose business it is, can possibly be, simply because he is capable of hearing, comprehending it. Why blink your own rhetoric? Why dont you go on and tell me it's for the good of my soul—if I have one?"[2]

Even before the long rigmarole of confession of sins, which constitutes what action there is, has been undertaken, all the characters are shown to be clearly aware of the real motives behind what ensues. Yet when the confession is over, and the governor has refused to grant a pardon, Faulkner still unbelievably attempts to sustain the narrative illusion that he forsook two hundred pages earlier.

The meaning, the message, is therefore all that is left to salvage from this weakest of Faulkner's novels. The qualities of allegory predominate here. Temple is everyman, the victim of environment, of tradition, of the evil of others. In *Sanctuary*, Temple was completely helpless in the grip of the forces of evil. There her name was as significant as it becomes in the sequel. The temple of the spirit, the body, is violated in *Sanctuary*. The human being, which is sacred in the Faulkner

---

[1] *Requiem for a Nun* (New York, 1951), 88.
[2] *Ibid.*, 90.

canon, is abused. In *Sanctuary,* Temple is a victim, and her
humanity is outrageously insulted by the complete disregard
for her dignity as a human being. In that novel she is used, like
something nonhuman, and there she symbolizes the victimiza-
tion of everyman at the hands of an inhuman, mechanistic
society symbolized by Popeye. In *Requiem,* her symbolic role
is reversed, and she learns how to purify the human temple by
the adherence to truth and a study of values. Here she symbolizes the alternative to the sickness and perversion of society
in the earlier novel.

As in *A Fable,* in the case of the runner, assistance is given
to everyman by a Christ-figure who exemplifies selflessness.
Nancy is such a figure. Nancy, like Christ, is executed on a
Friday (March 13). Nancy, moreover, accepts her sentence
willingly, without fear or regret. She creates chaos in the
courtroom by greeting her sentence with a righteous "Yes,
Lord."[3] Temple mimics this with an envious and bitter, but
accurate interpretation: "Yes, God. Guilty, God. Thank you,
God."[4]

Nancy receives her sentence as she does because it is exactly
what she sought. She views her death as necessary and inevitable and with placid resignation. She is the rare example
in Faulkner of the colored person, always the scapegoat, become active. The question of Nancy's role leads us to observe
the important third theme (there is no connotation of order
of importance intended) in the novel: the specifically Southern theme, which here, as elsewhere, symbolizes the universal
one. It is obviously not accident that it should be Nancy
whom Faulkner chooses as his Christ. That she is a Negro
is meaningful in terms of the attitude that Joanna Burden
has in *Light in August.* The latter believes that the Negro

[3] *Ibid.,* 51.
[4] *Ibid.,* 54.

race is the white man's cross. Since the Negro is a continual "thorn" of guilt in the white man's side, Nancy must be seen locally as well as universally. Her positive action here reflects ironically on her employer's failure. Moreover, she provides, as all of Faulkner's Negroes do, a chance for the white man to face his own guilt, ostensibly here to try to reprieve the Negro, but actually to be freed of the burden of guilt exactly as Chick Mallison is. Nancy, by her selfless murder of Temple's baby, has in a sense arrested time. She has stemmed the tide of evil, not only in this specific case which began in *Sanctuary*, but in the universal situation which began with civilization, represented in *Requiem* by the founding of Jefferson. By her act she enables Temple to change the course of her life and come to grips with reality and to terms with herself before God.

This is literally represented in morality-play fashion in the novel. The governor is God:

> The whole bottom of the stage is in darkness, as in Scene I, Act One, so that the visible scene has the effect of being held in the beam of a spotlight. Suspended too, since it is upper left and even higher above the shadow of the stage proper than the same in Scene I, Act One, carrying still further the symbolism of the still higher, the last, the ultimate seat of judgment . . . .
>
> The Governor stands in front of the high chair, between it and the desk, beneath the emblem on the wall. He is symbolic too: no known person, neither old nor young; he might be someone's idea not of God but of Gabriel perhaps, the Gabriel not before the Crucifixion but after it.[5]

God or Gabriel, it amounts to the same thing in the action of the novel. The allegory is further elaborated by Gavin Stevens, who serves as priest.[6] It is he who, pretending to have

[5] *Ibid.*, 112–13.
[6] Olga Vickery has elaborated on Gavin Stevens' function as a priest-figure

a legal interest in the case, persuades Temple, by a process of prodding her conscience and hounding her person, to confront the governor. Ostensibly sitting in judgment, the governor enables Temple to meet herself, to arrive at an awareness of her own predicament. The allegorical pattern may thus be summed up: Christ, or one such as Christ (this could mean in fact any totally committed humanist), causes a pause or break in the chain reaction of evil. The hard shell of illusion and indifference, defensively constructed by the individual, is thus shattered, and he is left bewildered but usefully disturbed; the priestly guide may then lead the individual to a confrontation with God, conceived of in this case as the overseer of justice or final authority on "truth"; having been led to desire truth, and thus to put the other before the self, man achieves the more important result of coming to moral integrity for himself, the result of self-awareness.

This allegorical meaning is emphasized by an accompanying history of Jefferson, both the town and the county. The relationship of the two distinct parts of *Requiem* is perhaps best illustrated by a comparison with another medium. A not uncommon film technique, used to convey the representative nature of the subject matter, is that of spanning with the camera an entire city or area before focusing in telescopic fashion upon one family or individual or apartment within the whole. The effect of this, as I have said, is to create the impression that the selected individual has been chosen at random, that he is only one of many, representing all. The history of Jefferson seems to span both time and space, and the history of Temple Drake appears to be an illustration of the general themes that are more skillfully implied in the prose sections.

in *Requiem.* "Gavin Stevens: from Rhetoric to Dialectic," *Faulkner Studies,* Vol. II (Spring, 1953), 1–4.

This element begins with the founding of Jefferson. It begins in what appears to be a trivial way, hardly worthy of mention. An individual named Holston owns a large lock, "fifteen pounds of useless iron,"[7] which is needlessly appended to the leather mail bag delivered to the town by a man named Pettigrew. The lock is borrowed to assist in the retention of some bandits who have been captured and brought to town. The bandits escape by removing an entire wall of the temporary jail, and the lock is lost forever. Holston demands his lock back, and Ratcliffe, a trader, suggests paying him fifteen or fifty dollars for the lock and charging the money to the Indian Bureau. Pettigrew, however, is the one to hinder this plan. He is an "ethical man." He cites laws to prevent this corruption, but Pettigrew himself is corruptible. His first name is Jefferson, and he is bribed with fame. The settlers agree to call their yet-to-be-built town Jefferson if Pettigrew will ignore the incident involving the lock. He agrees, and the first building of Jefferson is the courthouse.

Irony pervades the entire episode. Although the characters are apparently drawn sympathetically, one must not mistake this for the author's viewpoint; one must look at the implications, or the episode is meaningless. The presence of the "useless iron" in the first place is a commentary on the fallibility of man. The antidote to banditry is obviously not locks, as is demonstrated by the bandits' ability to dismantle the building itself:

> not just the lock gone from the door nor even just the door gone from the jail, but the entire wall gone, the mud-chinked axe-morticed logs unjointed neatly and quietly in the darkness and stacked as neatly to one side, leaving the jail open to the world like a stage.[8]

[7] *Requiem for a Nun*, 8.
[8] *Ibid.*, 16.

The orderly "breakdown" of civilization is not hindered by a lock. The fact that Pettigrew is an ethical man is interesting, and even more interesting is the fact that he can be corrupted by fame. Clearly an ethical man is not necessarily a man who loves truth. He is a man of the letter rather than the spirit, and Faulkner satirizes the type when he satirizes Pettigrew. The latter has memorized the rules:

> "Act of Congress as made and provided for the unauthorised removal and or use or willful or felonious use or misuse or loss of government property, penalty the value of the article plus five hundred to ten thousand dollars or thirty days to twenty years in a Federal jail or both."[9]

The courthouse is a living testimony to rule by letter rather than spirit, and it is ironic that an institution dedicated to the preservation of law should grow out of corruption. It is ironic, but it is not surprising, because the very establishment of laws and courthouse is a testimony to their inadequacy. The ineptness of the laws and their failure to meet the needs of society is amply demonstrated by Nancy's conflict with them. The law, the mechanics of society, are wallowing in one realm, and Nancy is living in another. Their ironic juxtaposition demonstrates the unreality of the contemporary answer to the needs of man.

But to return to Jefferson history, the final irony is provided by Faulkner's comment that Ratcliffe is troubled by the failure of the settlers to cheat the government out of the cost of the lock. Private individuals finally pay Holston for his lock, and Ratcliffe would try to explain the way he felt about it:

> It's like Old Moster and the rest of them up there that run the luck, would look down at us and say, Well well, looks like them durn peckerwoods down there dont want them fifteen dollars

9 *Ibid.*, 24–25.

we was going to give them free-gratis-for-nothing. So maybe they dont want nothing from us. So maybe we better do like they seem to want, and let them sweat and swivet and scrabble through the best they can by themselves.[10]

It is, of course, the scrabbling for himself that distinguishes man and makes him admirable in Faulkner's eyes. This first section of *Requiem*, as an isolated short story, is without doubt admirable. The characters emerge vividly from the imagination of their creator, and there is real dramatic action that carries the reader from beginning to end. Unfortunately, as we will see, the episode is certainly isolated in the novel.

The founding of Jefferson epitomizes the founding of civilization. The beginnings of society, of the enterprise of men in living together, is marred by the overshadowing symbolic presence of the lock. It represents a lack of trust, and the fact that it is useless and described as such by Faulkner indicates his view that man creates his own errors for, after all, it is man-made. The lock is a token of exclusiveness, but man at his best can be inclusive. Once, however, the seeds of evil are sown, their harvest is continual. The decay spreads through time. The evils of Jefferson become the evils of Jackson, a capital city. At each stage, Jefferson, Jackson, jail, and Temple, there is, however, the possibility of alternative. Man is continually given a choice.

The chapter on Jackson is for the most part unadulterated history, only occasionally enlivened even by the author's overt point of view:

. . . because then came the Anglo-Saxon, the pioneer, the tall man, roaring with Protestant scripture and boiled whiskey, Bible and jug in one hand and (like as not) a native tomahawk in the other, brawling, turbulent not through viciousness but simply

[10] *Ibid.*, 43.

Requiem for a Nun

because of his over-revved glands; uxorious and polygamous: a married invincible bachelor, dragging his gravid wife and most of the rest of his mother-in-law's family behind him into the trackless infested forest, spawning that child as like as not behind the barricade of a rifle-crotched log mapless leagues from nowhere and then getting her with another one before reaching his final itch-footed destination, and at the same time scattering his ebullient seed in a hundred dusky bellies through a thousand miles of wilderness; innocent and gullible, without bowels, for avarice or compassion or forethought either, changing the face of the earth: felling a tree which took two hundred years to grow, in order to extract from it a bear or a capful of wild honey.[11]

From such beginnings comes the capitol. But the real symbolic significance of the capitol can only be realized in connection with Temple's visit to the governor there. The capitol is a wayside point, a choosing place for good or evil in the history of man:

> . . . and in 1903 the new Capitol was completed—the golden dome, the knob, the gleamy crumb, the gilded pustule longer than the miasma and the gigantic ephemeral saurians, more durable than the ice and the pre-night cold, soaring, hanging as one blinding spheroid above the center of the Commonwealth, incapable of being either looked full or evaded, peremptory, irrefragible, and reassuring.[12]

Temple does look full at the capitol, going to its very heart, the source of justice, there to examine herself.

Temple and Nancy thus provide an ideal case in Faulkner's history of man, ideal in that they act as Faulkner would have us all act in order to stop the disintegration begun in symbolic Jefferson. Unfortunately, Temple is the exception, which is, of course, why the novel comes to be written. Jackson remains

[11] *Ibid.*, 102.
[12] *Ibid.*, 110.

the unwholesome conglomeration that Faulkner satirizes at the end of this section:

Transport: Street buses, Taxis.
Accommodations: Hotels, Tourist camps, Rooming houses.
Radio: WJDX, WTJS.
Diversions: chronic: S.I.A.A., Basketball Tournament, Music Festival, Junior Auxiliary Follies, May Day Festival, State Tennis Tournament, Red Cross Water Pageant, State Fair, Junior Auxiliary Style Show, Girl Scouts Horse Show, Feast of Carols.
Diversions: acute: Religion, Politics.[13]

There are accommodations, not homes; there is radio, but no communication, and the lists of diversions ought ideally to be reversed; surely religion and politics should be "chronic," not "acute." This line of evil, this sickness of society, began long ago and yet persists in the Jefferson of *Sanctuary*. This is the same Jefferson, now sicker than ever, harboring a Popeye, the subhuman species of total disintegration, impotent, black with sin. Yet even he, the "cockroach" of society, the epitome of evil, is in Faulkner's eyes a victim of his society. He is finally hanged for a crime he did not commit.

The total incompetence of society to judge itself is the subject matter of the last prose section of *Requiem*. Here, in a chapter entitled "The Jail," Faulkner goes to the core of the problem. The history of Jefferson's jail is given at length, from its beginnings to the present, when we find it housing Nancy. In the long section on the jail, with its attempt to indicate the speed of civic and technological progress, we find many senticious and bitter comments like the following:

And still—the old jail—endured, sitting in its rumorless cul-de-sac, its almost seasonless backwater in the middle of that rush

13 *Ibid.*, 111.

and roar of civic progress and social alteration and change . . . on the way out of course (to disappear from the surface of the earth along with the rest of the town on the day when all America, after cutting down all the trees and leveling the hills and mountains with bulldozers, would have to move underground to make room for, get out of the way of, the motor cars).[14]

We are being told that the failure of the new town to recognize and take note of the old jail is a failure of the present to look back in critical assessment. In an all-embracing indiscrimination, society absorbs all the weaknesses and failures of its past. Moreover, there is a growing lack of even ethical awareness. Everything is now tolerable, and the jail is best not regarded. But the jail is presented sympathetically, like a personage, and that is because it represents the perverted judgments that a valueless society makes about its members.

The jail, for two antithetical reasons, is the ideal symbol for Faulkner of a place of refuge and learning. It is, in the one case, the very earliest evidence of man's conscious knowledge of his own evil. By returning to it, one symbolically reexamines the source of evil, the process, in other words of repentance and renewal. On the other hand, by what we might call ironic inversion, the jail is the real place of refuge from a society which cannot judge itself. In the jail the wrong people, like Nancy, are always "crucified." This ironic attitude towards society is found in the inversion practiced by Blake when he praises the pleasant warmth of the ale house and condemns the cold sobriety of the church![15] Faulkner employs it elsewhere, for instance in "Uncle Willy," where the hero, a drug addict, wins our sympathy at the expense of the righteous church members. The persistent presence of the jail

[14] *Ibid.*, 247–48.
[15] "The Little Vagabond," *Complete Writings of William Blake* (London, 1957).

at the very center of the town, standing, like a nagging cancer, overgrown by progress, is a permanent reminder of man's incredible obtuseness in recognizing, but willfully refusing to eradicate, his own evil. This is what the jail means in Faulkner's fiction. Temple, having been directed now to the means, having been cleansed, prepared, goes to the jail to learn, consolidate, and understand.

To summarize the meaning of *Requiem* as a whole is to repeat Faulkner's humanistic thesis. People have responsibility to themselves and to each other. When Gowan says, "A child, and a dope-fiend nigger whore on a public gallows: that's all I had to pay for immunity," Stevens replies, "There's no such thing."[16] There is no immunity, no isolation, only the brotherhood of man. To face reality, to see the inescapable oneness of man, must be the principal object of the individual imagination. This task is made more difficult by the integrated nature of time. As Stevens says, "The past is never dead. It's not even past."[17] This echoes the similarly cryptic truism in *Intruder*. Because of this, one must face the extremely difficult problem of persistently examining one's own values. Temple, who has naturally lost faith in humanity after her experiences in *Sanctuary*, finds this more difficult than most: "I'm trying. I'm really trying. Maybe it wouldn't be so hard if I could just understand why they dont stink—what reason they would have for not stinking."[18] But Temple, with Nancy's help, does come to grips with the problem of herself, for she herself is society. Even Temple can do this; for most men, therefore, there ought certainly to be hope!

The problem of style here is one that must be given careful consideration. The styles of the two parts of *Requiem*, or at

16 *Requiem for a Nun*, 71.
17 *Ibid.*, 92.
18 *Ibid.*, 65.

least the motives that produce those styles are not very different. I have already commented on the failure of the characters to be anything but spokesmen for their creator. To elaborate on this, one must again resort to the distinction between symbol and allegory. The allegorical emblem becomes echoing symbol when it becomes complex enough to be real. The people in this novel have no depth; they are not fully realized. There is no care in their presentation. There is no normal dialogue in any of the three acts of the play; sententious observation is substituted for conversation. The characters never really want or try to communicate; they speak only to give utterance to an idea or to clarify something to themselves. Gavin Stevens at one point quotes the governor's refusal to pardon Nancy:

> Who am I, to have the brazen temerity and hardihood to set the puny appanage of my office in the balance against that simple undeviable aim: Who am I, to render null and abrogate the purchase she made with that poor crazed lost and worthless life![19]

This is not speech, but a speech, and Faulkner had permitted himself to write in this way only since 1948. The above reminds us of its twin in *A Fable*, when the General says:

> If he does, if he accepts his life, keeps his life, he will have abrogated his own gesture and martyrdom. If I gave him his life tonight, I myself could render null and void what you call the hope and the dream of his sacrifice. By destroying his life tomorrow morning, I will establish forever that he didn't even live in vain, let alone die so. Now tell me who's afraid?[20]

Two gods pronounce sentence on two Christs. Faulkner's most recent novels have asserted values, answers to human problems, that were once implied in the structure of his earlier writings.

[19] *Ibid.*, 210. [20] *A Fable* (New York, 1950), 332.

The special faculty of the great novelist, that which makes him a poet-novelist, is the ability to see at once, in a kind of vision, his point of view represented in a metaphor. The great novel is a giant image. Thus, with Faulkner, his greatest success is found in his simplest plots. In *The Sound and the Fury* we find a family representing the family of man, and the disintegration of the one is a metaphor for the breakdown of the other. Again, in *As I Lay Dying*, the journey of life is embodied in a real pilgrimage towards burial. The best metaphors must treat of symbols that have implicit universal application. Throughout literature one finds the great symbols repeated because they are already, perhaps unconsciously, part of the reader's own creative understanding: the family, the journey, a house, a hunt, a trial, a birth, and so on. Once the writer, failing to visualize the metaphor for his "message," tries to conjure up with his reason a contrived setting which will "do" for his idea, the result will be stilted and unimaginative.

We might well define rhetoric in fiction as the use of an ornate, self-conscious, and pompous verbiage which makes no real contribution to the matter of which it treats. Thus the prose in *Absalom, Absalom!* and *The Sound and the Fury* is not rhetorical because it makes a specific and vital contribution to the analysis of states of mind, of which the matter of those novels is largely constituted. *Intruder in the Dust*, *A Fable*, and *Requiem for a Nun*, on the other hand, are highly rhetorical, because the prose style employed in those novels is of no particular value. In a straightforward description by an omniscient author, simple unadorned prose would appear to serve as well as any other. The aim of such description is presumably to bring the object and the reader as close to each other as possible through words. When the words become unfamiliar and the syntax a tangled maze, what results is a chasm rather than a bridge. The words chosen should subordinate themselves to the picture they evoke, and if they do not, if they assert themselves like a barrier between reader and object, the writer has failed.

Two examples will serve to demonstrate the line that must be drawn between useful elaboration and rhetoric. Both of the following passages I believe to be characteristic of the novels from which they are taken.

> Memory believes before knowing remembers. Believes longer than recollects, longer than knowing even wonders. Knows remembers believes a corridor in a big long garbled cold echoing building of dark red brick sootbleakened by more chimneys than its own, set in a grassless cinder-strewnpacked compound surrounded by smoking factory purlieus and enclosed by a ten foot steel-and-wire fence like a penitentiary or a zoo, where in random erratic surges, with sparrowlike child-trebling, orphans in identical and uniform blue denim in and out of remembering but in knowing constant as the bleak walls, the bleak windows where in rain soot from the yearly adjacenting chimneys streaked like black tears.[21]

> In the beginning was already decreed this rounded knob, this gilded pustule, already before and beyond the steamy chiaroscuro, untimed unseasoned winterless miasma not any one of water or earth or life yet all of each, inextricable and indivisible; that one seethe one spawn one motherwomb, one furious tumescence, father-mother-one, one vast incubant ejaculation already fissionating in one boiling moil of litter from the celestial experimental Work Bench; that one spawning crawl and creep printing with three-toed mastodonic tracks the steamy-green swaddling clothes of the coal and the oil, above which the peabrained reptilian heads curved the heavy leather-flapped air.[22]

[21] *Light in August*, 111.
[22] *Requiem for a Nun*, 99.

The characteristics of the vocabulary are essentially the same. The difference in the passages lies in their application. The first is a painfully serious effort to reveal the background and coloring, the elements, that went together to produce Joe Christmas. The description is a vital, integral part of the narrative itself. In the second case, the description is set in isolation. It has no connection with anything, except by the most tenuous of threads, and, therefore, it is difficult to see what justification there is for the particular choice of words and syntax.

Harvey Breit, in his introduction to *Absalom, Absalom!* in the Modern Library edition, says of the prose that it is "oblique, involuted, circumambient; the language is spectacular, a conglomerate; and both the vision and the words are directed (driven would be more exact) by an honesty that is uncompromising and difficult."[23] In the passage from *Light in August*, the author is honestly trying to unwind and unravel time in order to search back into the nuances of his hero's creation. In the description from *Requiem*, Faulkner is trying to reveal the intensity of his own visualization of the prehistoric past. The first meets the demands of fiction, the second meets the demands of the author's need for self-expression; the first is characterized by artistic control, the second by a lack of it. This is not to say that the second is not skillful. It is. But the difference between these two passages is the difference between the total unity and single focus in a novel like *Light in August*, and the confusion of purpose that results from the loss of the over-all imaginative impetus in *Requiem for a Nun* and *Intruder in the Dust*.

[23] William Faulkner, *Absalom, Absalom!* (New York, 1936, 1951), v.

CHAPTER VI

A Fable
"You'll put your own ideas in his mouth"

F aulkner's decision to leave his old, familiar subject matter and turn to foreign material in *A Fable* can be accounted for only by his increasing desire to place before an ever larger audience the most patently obvious rendering of his single vision. World War I is a setting that appealed to him because it was a world war, a conflict in which all were involved, directly or by proxy, and it conveniently accorded with Faulkner's desire to speak to a "world" audience on subjects that were significant to the "world." That is why Faulkner could not choose the Amercian Civil War, and that is why he could no longer rest content in the comfortable familiarity of Yoknapatawpha County, where he had always been most at home. Faulkner himself accounts for *A Fable* in this way:

> To tell that story, the thought was if I could just tell this in such a powerful way that people will read it and say this must not happen again, that is, if Providence, Deity, call Him what you will, had tried to save this world once, save men once by the sacrifice of His Son, that failed, He tried it again and that failed, maybe He wouldn't try it the third time, and so we must take warning because He may not try to save us again that way.[1]

But Faulkner failed to see that universality in fiction is not necessarily attained by writing about the "biggest" events, nor can the writer guarantee the most powerful presentation of his ideas simply by stating them as baldly as possible. By

[1] *Nagano*, 159.

111

seeking to employ the Christian myth, Faulkner sought to speak to hearts already receptive to his morality, to find that vast Western audience already weaned on Christian love and doctrine and thus able and willing to accept the tough diet which he planned to offer them. The idea might have seemed sound enough to a man whose desire for such communication was urgent. But Faulkner did not take into account the elements of fiction along with the demands of his thesis. He could not see the consequences pursuant upon his desire to preach, and he was unable to predict that powerful convictions are no assurance of equally powerful images through which to present them. The Nobel Prize was awarded in 1950, and its accompanying address and some earlier fiction might have warned us that the subject matter of *A Fable* (1954) could very well come after. But so tortured is the style of *A Fable* and so sententious and forthright its point of view that only now can we speculate on the significance which the universal recognition of the Nobel Prize must have had for Faulkner. It is a great temptation now to suggest that Faulkner's real loss of creative power since the thirties had nothing to do with age or money or even recognition; rather it is the result of his own self-consciousness growing out of a new-found realization that he had a vast audience; the consequent burden of responsibility, which such a morally committed author must have, may well have resulted in a subverting of imagination to the demands of a dialectic. Whether this is so or not, *A Fable* is the climax of an increasing tendency towards the allegorical presentation of moral sentiment that is visible in the later work of Faulkner, but is nowhere else so obvious.

The story of *A Fable* revolves around the disaffection of a regiment of the French Army in France during World War I. Commanded to attack under the leadership of a General Gragnon, they refuse. The Germans take no advantage of this situation, indicating that they too have decided to reject war. The mutiny is primarily the achievement of a corporal and twelve close comrades, who for some time have been infiltrating throughout their own and even the enemy lines, inspiring pacificism. The mutiny causes a temporary cessation of the war which lasts the brief time span of the novel; during this pause the fate of the thirteen arrested ringleaders is in the balance.

The plot of *A Fable* is built on the opposition of the military authorities (the forces of war) to the men in the ranks who make the bid for peace. This antipathy is the impulse for most of the events following the mutiny. Because of the crisis, the supreme generals of the four involved armies meet together. This is in itself a sign of the vast deceit which the men oppose. The presence of the German general at this meeting is necessary to the continuation of the war. Peace, now achieved very simply, is not attractive to the forces of authority who see the struggle in abstract terms, rather than as a conflict between men. In this way the meeting symbolizes evil for three principal characters in the novel. One learns from it that man is being ruthlessly exploited under cover of abstract nouns like glory, honor, and motherland. Another learns to recognize that evil is still a constituent of the human character and that man persistently undermines his godliness, and a third learns that there is hope for man as long as he can provoke such opposition as the meeting demonstrates.

A greater urgency is given to the implications of these events by an allegorical parallel to the days of the last week in the life of Christ. For instance, the peace plot is revealed to the authorities by a betrayer who, like Judas, is a member of the guilty regiment. The corporal who devises the scheme presides at a final supper on the eve of his execution; he is shot as he stands tied to a post between two thieves, likewise executed; he dies with his head in a "crown" of barbed wire, and he is "resurrected." His father is the very general responsible for his death, as well as for his birth. He is also the tempter who offers the corporal life and power. These are only a few of the references in the novel to the events of the New Testament. The importance of this allegory lies not in the unnecessary retelling of the well-known events for the sake of ingenuity, but in the particular interpretation of the myth which Faulkner here dramatizes.

This interpretation is best indicated by the ironic last chapter called "Tomorrow." Twelve soldiers, led by a sergeant, undertake a journey to find a suitable candidate for the title of "Unknown Soldier." After a brandy-sodden expedition and a descent underground into the place of the dead, they make a drunken return with a corpse. Desperate for liquor, however, they sell the corpse to a deluded old woman, who claims it as her son. Corpseless, they awake from a drunken stupor, sobered into a realization of the enormity of their offense and forced to bargain with a farmer for a corpse that he has found on his land.

The body is that of the corporal, disinterred by an explosion from its original grave and thrown into a neighboring field. The soldiers purchase the body with a watch and return with it to Paris. Christ, by a freak accident, now fills the grave of the Unknown Soldier. The irony of this situation is complex. The Unknown Soldier is a figure designed to commemorate every dead soldier, which in the military context of this novel, means the commemoration of everyman. Heroism is the attribute of this national monument, yet obscurity is its principal characteristic. Christ reappears unexpectedly as a "last resort" for the searchers, but He then assumes the above characteristics of a deliberately obscured fame. Faulkner seems to be saying that the fate of Christ in the society of man is to

be always present but never recognized. Christ is thus metaphorically entombed in the midst of a bustling society.

The drunken journey represents the traditional life journey—this time the pointless existence, the "quiet desperation"
of most men. The selling of the body for brandy is the attempt
to forget the inevitability of death, of reality. It is an attempt
to sell death by buying oblivion. But any oblivion that can
be bought is only temporary. Although the soldiers are unaware of the significance of the purchase of the second corpse,
we are meant to see the exchange as a metaphor for the solution of the human problem. We must have some belief, and a
belief in the Christian ethic is the best Faulkner can offer.
The watch that is surrendered in exchange for the body of
the corporal symbolizes the meaningless abstractions, like
linear time, that dominate the lives of most men in the twentieth century.

In *The Sound and the Fury,* Jason and Quentin are both
concerned with clocks, which represent a pettiness and im-
mediacy or a concern with the past that is unsatisfying as a
way of living. Dilsey, however, is able to understand the in-
accurate kitchen clock. She is not dominated by the passage
of time. So the soldiers make the only exchange that will lead
to the acceptance of Christ in society. The awakening and the
consequent purchase of the body of Christ with a watch is
Faulkner's reminder that there is an alternative to the oppressive meaninglessness of a life without values. Man can throw
over the bonds of time, the dreadful concern with the heavy
approach of death, by belief.

Translated into nonsymbolic terms, the entire episode indicates that everyman fails to recognize himself—that is, the
potential within himself—and fails to be the full man of peace
and goodness Christ is. It would hardly be exaggerating to say
that any and every man can be Christ, the humanist Christ,

the son and epitome of man that Faulkner has extracted from the New Testament. For Faulkner the power of the gospel lies in the God-man unity represented therein. This accounts for his attempt to rationalize the miracles into exemplifications of humanitarianism. The power of the Christ-story lies, not in its mystic aspects, but in its metaphor about the nature of man. The crucifying of Christ is the picture of man crucifying himself—making a deliberate choice to eliminate that part of himself that partakes of divinity.

This duality of man's nature, symbolized by the conflict between the mass and Christ, lies at the heart of *A Fable*. It is a conflict between collective man and the usual consciousness of the individual. Faulkner is preaching that Christ is ever with us and may at any time be resurrected, or in other words, that man is continuously faced with the responsibility of choosing between good and evil and must take the consequences of his choice.

In a review of *A Fable*, Vivian Mercier suggests that the symbols of the gospels "must, for Christians, in the last analysis embody a superhuman reality."[2] The implicit irony of this comment is that it denies by assertion the possibility of the humanistic interpretation of the gospels that Faulkner wishes to make. Faulkner's interpretation may not be the orthodox one, but in *A Fable* he is advocating Christian ethics, and he is urging the spirit of Christ's commandments.

ii

The French regiment under the command of General Gragnon is ordered on Monday to make a futile attack but, instead of doing so, mutinies. Upon the consequent failure of the Germans to utilize the Allies' weakness to their own advan-

[2] "Search for Universality That Led Too Far from Home," *Commonweal*, Vol. LX (August 6, 1954), 444.

tage, a meeting (of the four commanders of the Allied and German armies) is arranged and held. Their problem is a common one: how to overcome the momentary dominance of man's best impulse and continue the war. The presence of the German general at such a meeting is, of course, heavily ironic. It clearly indicates that the war is a game, that the opposing generals have more closely identified aims than does any general and his own army. The presence of the German general on this occasion is the sign of the evil of the war and so, by implication, of Evil itself. It signifies the denial of any possible meaning through the service of those abstract nouns under cover of which the war is being justified: honor, glory, freedom, truth, etc.

Gerald Levine joins the war as a pilot because of his infatuation with the sound of these empty abstractions. Not many days after his enlistment the mutiny occurs, and the German general lands at the aerodrome where Levine is stationed. He had entered the war with a schoolboy's illusion. The word that dominates his thinking is "glory." Levine has involved himself in the war in order to become a hero, to establish himself in the "Valhalla" of British warriors, to be the flying ace that every child in the West had dreamed of being. That all these ideas are part of Levine's immaturity is emphasized throughout:

> He jumped down to the tarmac, already running, so young in breathing that he wouldn't be nineteen for another year and yet so young in war that, although the Royal Air Force was only six weeks old, his was not the universal tunic with RFC badges super-posed on the remnants of old regimental insigne which veteran transfers wore, and he didn't even own the old official Flying Corps tunic at all: his was the new RAF thing not only unmartial but even a little epicene, with its cloth belt

and no shoulderstraps like the coat of the adult leader of a neo-Christian boys' club.[3]

In the total structure of the novel Faulkner symbolizes various existent and possible outlooks by the personification of reactions to the discovery of evil. In this sense, Levine is characterized by moral immaturity. As a paradigm of human naïveté, the Levine episode assumes significance for the meaning of the novel as a whole.

On joining the air corps, the boy had ignored the wishes of his widowed mother.

> [He had been] gazetted not into the RFC but into the RAF. Because the RFC had ceased to exist on April Fool's day, two days before his commission came through: whereupon that March midnight had seemed to him a knell. A door had closed on glory; immortality itself had died in unprimered anti-climax: not his to be the old commission in the old glorious corps, the brotherhood of heroes to which he had dedicated himself even at the cost of that wrench to his mother's heart.[4]

He has forsaken mother for motherland—exchanged real human relationships for unreal abstractions. On more than one occasion he is called "the child." For Faulkner awareness of reality is largely an awareness of the evil of an unquestioned tradition or of the abstractions that dominate contemporary attitudes. Like Quentin Compson, Levine is unable to face reality—unable to cope with the discovery of evil. A child apparently accepts imposed standards, but is unable to assume the responsibility for considering the existential implications of these standards. Man, however, must be willing to face such responsibility. In *The Sound and the Fury*, Quentin, depending on a tradition which no longer has any validity (and

[3] *A Fable*, 87–88.
[4] *Ibid.*, 88.

which, in fact, was always based on an illusion), is unequipped to accept, absorb, and adjust to the discovery of evil (reality), symbolized by the promiscuity of his sister. He commits suicide because he is unable to live in the real world. Levine finally takes his own life for the same reason. He, too, finds himself inadequately equipped to meet the demands of reality.

To live with such a discovery as he makes, Levine would have needed a strong moral perception, an ability to balance evil with good, to estimate the relativity of things. Instead he has inherited a false tradition which glorifies war and lauds abstractions, which is proven false by the appearance of the German general. Faulkner satirizes Levine's view of the past:

> Their inheritors—Bishop and Mannock and Voss and McCudden and Fonck and Barker and Richthofen and Nungesser— would still cleave the earth-foundationed air, pacing their fleeing shadows on the scudding canyon-walls of cumulae, furloughed and immune, secure in immortality even while they still breathed, but it would not be his. Glory and valor would still exist of course as long as men lived to reap them. It would even be the same valor in fact, but the glory would be another glory. And that would be his: some second form of Elysium, a cut above dead infantry perhaps, but little more: who was not the first to think *What had I done for motherland's glory had motherland but matched me with her need.*[5]

His unrealizable wish to serve motherland is clearly intended to provide ironic comment on his refusal to serve his real mother, who is otherwise needlessly dragged into the episode.

Levine's character and moral strength are further brought into question in the description of his encounter with silence:

> He went out into the darkness, the silence, walking on in the

[5] *Ibid.,* 89.

direction of the huts as long as anyone from the mess might still see him, then giving himself another twenty steps for good measure before he turned away toward the hangars, thinking how his trouble was probably very simple, really: he had never heard silence before; he had been thirteen, almost fourteen, when the guns began, but perhaps even at fourteen you still could not bear silence: you denied it at once and immediately began to try to do something about it as children of six or ten do: as a last resort, when even noise failed, fleeing into closets, cupboards, corners under beds or pianos, lacking any other closeness and darkness in which to escape it.[6]

Since here the silence means for Levine the absence of the war (the constant shelling has momentarily stopped), silence must be the symbolic equivalent of a moral vacuum. The compulsion of the child to fill silence with noise and thus banish it is like the need of the adult to fill the moral void upon discovering it. Levine finds, upon the arrival of the German general, that all his illusions were false and baseless; his world falls apart for lack of solid foundations, and he is faced with the need to cope with the ensuing nothingness. Understanding precedes the responsibility of choice. Choosing requires certain skills or abilities. Levine is not equipped to weigh the possibilities pursuant upon knowledge.

In order to perpetrate the war deceit, to draw the wool over the eyes of man, the authorities provide a display of dummy gunfire when the aeroplane of the German general approaches the Allied lines. To prove to himself that his disillusion is well founded, Levine insists that Bridesman, his flight commander, fire at him the substituted ammunition.[7] In other words, Levine is willing to stake his life on the "reality" of the principles for which he believes the war is being fought. Iron-

[6] *Ibid.*, 95–96.

[7] The name here is, of course, deliberately chosen to signify that the flight commander is attendant on the moral virgin.

ically, should his faith in the military propaganda be well founded, should the bullets be real, he will die happily; should they be false, he will live miserably. The result is that while his body remains unharmed, his Sidcott begins to smolder. It burns itself away over twenty-four hours while Levine carefully nurses its disintegration. It is the symbol of his illusion of glory, and upon its death he must die too. He commits suicide in the latrine.

But before he dies, his thoughts indicate that he has come to an awareness that any service he might have been able to offer England, even if he had become the hero of his dreams, would have had no ultimate significance. The strength of a nation does not in fact rest on Levine's illusions.

> And then he knew that it really didn't matter, not to England: Lundendorff could come on over Amiens and turn for the coast and get into his boats and cross the Channel and storm whatever he thought fit between Goodwin Sands and Land's End and Bishop's Rock and take London too and it wouldn't matter. Because London signified England as the foam signifies the beer, but the foam is not the beer and nobody would waste much time or breath grieving, nor would Ludendorff have time to breathe either or spend gloating, because he would still have to envelop and reduce every tree in every wood and every stone in every wall in all England, not to mention three men in every pub that he would have to tear down brick by brick to get to them. And it would not matter when he did, because there would be another pub at the next crossroads with three more men in it and there were simply just not that many Germans nor anybody else in Europe or anywhere else, and he unrolled the Sidcott.[8]

Here Faulkner offers one of many statements about human endurance. What distinguishes man is his being human, his humble dedication to the realities of a gloryless domestic

[8] *A Fable*, 119–20.

existence, his ties with home, family, and his encounter with and absorption of sorrow, grief, and joy.

Throughout Faulkner's work man is represented as both innocent and guilty. He is innocent of his past and guilty if he shapes the future irresponsibly. Unable to regulate either the values thrust upon him or his environment, he is, nevertheless, responsible for his own integrity, which involves examining the validity of the society to which he vocally or silently subscribes. Man is thus faced with the need to discover a set of values, references fixed in the midst of confusion. The corporal personifies these values. Levine is shown as a symbol of "uncharted" man. He has failed to achieve moral maturity, and his suicide is the final comment on his thorough weakness.

iii

The second of two socially prevalent and destructive attitudes is embodied in the Norman. He is shown as a weak and physically sick man. He has spent his life in a false hoping, in an unfounded believing. He has failed to face the responsibility of the individual. Where Levine worships words, the Norman puts his faith in some other person. In his dedication to an inactive faith in God, he clearly resembles the ascetic monk who removes himself from the real world, convinced of the sufficiency of faith and ignorant of the humanistic implications involved in being man. The Norman, when we meet him in the novel, is a quartermaster general. He attended the military school of St. Cyr along with the old general. The latter came from a background of power, influence, and wealth. The Norman had none of these advantages, yet he is second only to the nameless general in his achievements. Both attained their notable records through sheer ability. Their early intimacy is essential to later events. At that time, in school, the Norman was the only associate of the general to comprehend the exceptional nature of his superior. Later, after he has suffered disillusionment, the Norman recalls his attitude:

> Because I didn't just believe in you, I loved you. I believed from that first moment when I saw you in that gate that day forty-seven years ago that you had been destined to save us. That you were chosen by destiny out of the paradox of your background, to be a paradox to your past in order to be free of human past to be the one out of all earth to be free of the compulsions of fear and weakness and doubt which render the rest of us incapable of what you were competent for; that you in your strength would even absolve us of our failure due to our weakness and fears.[9]

In the course of the novel we learn that the old general is the father of the corporal as a result of an illicit affair in his youth. In terms of the New Testament allegory this naturally equates the general with God. We will examine the details of this equation later, but for the moment it is necessary to bear it in mind in order to comprehend the meaning of the Norman's point of view.

As we have seen, the Norman has placed all his faith and hope in the general's ability to save man. As a result of this belief, the Norman suffers three distinct disillusionments, culminating in a final and lasting comprehension and grief. He experiences his first disappointment and the first blow to his faith in the general when he learns about an incident at a desert outpost over which the general had charge. One of the legionnaires, a murderer, repeats his old crime by murdering an Arab slave girl and stealing a camel. The Riff band demands the surrender of the man and threatens otherwise the

[9] *Ibid.*, 328.

destruction of the garrison. A volunteer is called for to bring outside help to the French post. The murderer volunteers, and the general knowingly permits the man to fall into the hands of a Riff ambush, as a consequence of which the man suffers a lingering death and is buried the next day. When he learns of this incident, the Norman tries to excuse the action by invoking in his own mind the general's tender years at the time—"using the two 'he's' indiscriminantely, as though the nurse too knew: 'Yes, he was a man. But he was young then, not much more than a child. These tears are not anguish: only grief.' "[10]

The second disappointment is the discovery of the German general's presence at the meeting of authority where strategy against the corporal is planned. The third is the knowledge that the general had authorized the shelling of a second peace group, clearly a disciple group of the corporal's, as they met unarmed an unarmed German group in No Man's Land. Finally, the Norman confronts the old general with a grieving accusation and offers his resignation. It is refused. At this point the Norman learns the truth from his superior.

In order to understand this truth fully, we must turn from the narrative to consider the old general. His predominant characteristic is his flexibility, his accessibility to man. He is, it is true, in a position of supreme power, and yet he always offers a man a choice. Nowhere is his action shown to be arbitrary. In the case of the desert murder he asked for a *volunteer* and merely acceded to the man's wish to put himself into the hazard. In the case of the corporal he offers life, wealth, and power, but the corporal chooses death. It is, I think, impossible to overestimate the importance of this pliability.

With this in mind, let us look again at the scene of the

[10] *Ibid.*, 271.

Norman's resignation. He explains his past faith and love and his disappointment. He accuses the old general of betraying his potential for saving man. Then the general points out that it was only because of one Polchek, who betrayed the plot, that the authorities ever learned of the peace bid. In other words, the forces of war and evil would have been helpless in the face of a united group. By extension, this unity of man refers also to the individual. Everyman is both a corporal and a Polchek. When he learns this, the Norman suffers the breakdown of the too-simple world that he, like Levine, had created. He has put all his faith in his "God" and ignored the responsibility of man. The deaths of the murderer, the corporal, the men in No Man's Land are all crucifixions, martyrdoms chosen by those men. The corporal and the general are both aware that only in death does the gesture of the son become validated. The Norman learns that he, along with everyone else, must accept the responsibility for the corporal's death. Everyman is responsible for his own integrity or his own crucifixion, the death of the Christ in him. The external act of crucifying the corporal mirrors the internal act of the crucifiers in crushing the corporal in themselves. This complex metaphor is best illustrated by a diagram.

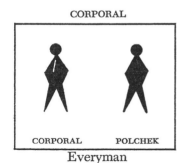 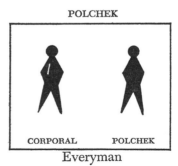

EVERYMAN IS BOTH A CORPORAL AND A POLCHEK

WILLIAM FAULKNER

MAN ACTS AGAINST MAN THEREFORE
MAN ACTS AGAINST HIMSELF

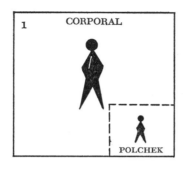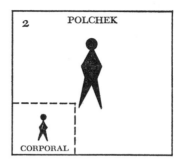

1. Corporal refuses to yield his integrity even at the cost of his life.

2. Polchek betrays corporal and causes his sacrifice.

As may be seen from the above diagram, man's social action reflects his inner situation. The state of society is merely the external and physical result of the many individuals' spiritual situations. Society takes whatever shape it does only through the decisions or absence of decisions of individuals. In so far as the corporal predominates, the Polchek is reduced, even to the point of elimination and vice versa.

iv

The runner represents the third reaction to evil or reality. Whereas both the pilot and the Norman move from illusion to disillusion and loss of faith, the runner is first encountered in the grip of disillusion. At the beginning of his story, he has reached the stage of despair and can only move towards the recovery of faith. His story begins with his application for release from his commission. He believes that man is voluntarily placing himself in the situation in which the war finds him. The runner is aware of evil, of the horror of the war, and so he refuses to accept any responsibility for the plight of man. At one point, an officer tells him, "If you really hate man all you need do is take your pistol back to the latrines and rid yourself of him."[11] He is being offered the exit that Levine chooses. The runner is not Levine. He rejects suicide. He does not really hate man; he really loves man, and his anguish is a result of his disappointment in what he loves.

Since his application for the removal of his commission has been refused, he hires a woman to commit with him a public indecency, and the authorities are tricked into lowering his rank. His subsequent choice of occupation is symbolic; he elects, as a private, to be a runner, a news-carrier, or in the context of the novel, a disciple. From the time of his return to the ranks the dynamic restoration of faith is the subject of the runner's story. But the story of the runner is also the story of another private, the groom, since the significance of each, both technically and symbolically, is dependent on the other. The runner becomes aware that in some way this other private has all the men of the battalion in his power. He lends them money and charges high interest. As security he holds their life-insurance policies. He makes money if they live, but more money if they die. The groom may thus be said ironically to control both their life and their death. When asked what some of the men must be paying the private, an officer replies, "Their souls obviously."[12] The symbolic picture painted here is of the devil, Old Harry (that is his name), binding the souls of men with and to materialism.

In order to know more about the groom, the runner also borrows money from him. There is symbolic implication in the runner's willingness to join the materialists temporarily.

[11] *Ibid.*, 65.
[12] *Ibid.*, 58.

This is one more indication of the runner's ability to face reality and then, as we shall see, to alter it. He observes of the groom:

> He has ethics, like a banker, not to his clients because they are people, but because they are clients. Not pity: he would bankrupt any—all—of them without turning a hair, once they had accepted the gambit; it's ethics toward his vocation, his trade, his profession.[13]

He is the pure materialist. To learn about his past, the runner pays a visit to one who knows the groom, the Reverend Tobe Sutterfield, a Negro minister who has set up in Paris a kind of association of grief, *"Les amis myriades et anonymes à la France de tout le monde."* The Reverend now calls himself Tooleyman—*Tout le Monde.* He represents the grieving world; he waits for man's readiness for conversion to goodness.

From this character the runner learns of the moneylender's past. He was once a groom. The horse that he attended was purchased and taken to South America first, and then to the United States, and the groom went as the only person who could satisfactorily handle the animal:

> It was 1912, two years before the war; the horse was a three-year-old running horse, but such a horse that even the price which the Argentine hide-and-wheat prince paid for it at the Newmarket sale, although an exceptional one, was not an outrageous one. Its groom was the sentry, the man with the ledger and the money-belt. He went out to America with it, whereupon within the next twenty-four months three things happened to him which changed completely not only his life, but his character too, so that when late in 1914 he returned to England to enlist, it was as though somewhere behind the Mississippi Valley hinterland where within the first three months he had vanished a new

13 *Ibid.,* 147.

man had been born, without past, without griefs, without recollections.[14]

The horse in question is no ordinary horse, however:

> "The horse," the old Negro said. "That they claimed we stole. Except that we couldn't have stole it, even if we had wanted to. Because it never belonged to no man to be stole from. It was the world's horse. The champion. No, that's wrong too. Things belonged to it, not it to things. Things and people both. He did. I did. All three of us did before it was over."[15]

The groom and Sutterfield are traveling through the South with the horse when their train is wrecked and the animal breaks a leg. Nothing daunted, they undertake to race it throughout the South, the objects of a gigantic, but for a long time futile chase. A reward is put upon their capture. It is believed that they have won vast sums of money. Finally, capture becomes inevitable, and the groom shoots the horse, whereupon it is discovered that they have no money at all. Money was apparently not the object of the racing. The deputy employed to defend the groom surmises that the latter must have shot the horse rather than "have it taken back to the Kentucky farm and shut it up in a whorehouse"[16]—rather than have it used for stud, reduced to the ignominy of such an occupation.

At this point we become convinced that the story has no validity except as a symbolic morality. The groom had dedicated himself to a horse to whom "things belonged." It is a three-legged yet unbeatable horse. It must surely represent an image of the Trinity, or of God. It is also presumably an Ideal, carried to America accompanied by the idealist groom. But because of greed, of commerce, the groom must kill the horse to preserve its integrity—it cannot live in such a society.

[14] *Ibid.*, 151.   [15] *Ibid.*, 150.   [16] *Ibid.*, 163.

Then the groom undergoes a profound change. He adopts the standards of the society in which he finds himself and returns to Europe as the champion of money, the king of materialism. He subjects men to the working of money. He becomes in fact, as his name indicates, Old Harry, the devil, fallen from Grace. The story may be viewed as a metaphor of the death of that promise which accompanied the foundation of a new society in the New World. America provided a fresh opportunity for man to demonstrate his capacity for love. The eighteenth-century humanism that pervades the Declaration of Independence, the Constitution, and the Bill of Rights gave a promise of enlightenment that was never fulfilled, and the values of a later America have moved from man to money.

Looked at in another way, the horse story is the more universal metaphor of the murder of God through the worship of things. By learning the story and confronting its symbolic implications, the runner is able to put things into perspective, is able to adjust to evil and realize its antidote. He now recognizes the groom as his archenemy, as the main obstacle in winning man to the side of peace and good. By overcoming Old Harry, the allegorical representation of Mammon, the runner can release man from his contract with materialism.

However, he does not undertake the contest with the groom until he is convinced of the action of the French regiment. "It's not that I don't believe," he says. "It's because it can't be true. We can't be saved now. Even He does not want us now."[17] By virtue of his job he learns early of the disaffection of the French troop. He sees that this is a giant step in the moral growth of man, and he responds with a renewal of faith:

> You can go out there now, at least during the next fifteen minutes, say, and not die probably. Yes, that may be the novelty: you can go out there now and stand erect and look about you—

[17] *Ibid.*, 69.

granted of course that any of us really ever can stand erect again. But we will learn how.[18]

The final step in his return is the discovery of the visit of the German general. In an episode pregnant with irony, Levine, proving to himself on his last mission that the bullets in his gun are not real, dives and fires at the runner. The latter's uniform catches fire, but unlike Levine's it becomes for him a symbol of joy. It is sufficient proof of man's strength, that he has forced the generals to such an expedient. It is proof of the success of the French mutiny. "It was enough."[19]

Whereas earlier the runner refused responsibility, he finally accepts it, without need of formal rank. He takes over the fate of his battalion by leading them unarmed into no man's land, forcing the groom to join them. The Germans, likewise without arms, meet them, but both forces are shelled by their own artillery.

"No!" he cried, "no! Not to us!" not even realising that he had said "we" and not "I" for the first time in his life probably, certainly for the first time in four years, not even realising that in the next moment he had said "I" again shouting to the old Negro as he whirled about: "What did I tell you? Didn't I tell you to let me alone?" Only it was not the old Negro, it was the runner, standing facing him as the first ranging burst of shells bracketed in.[20]

Along with his faith, the runner survives to make a dramatic reappearance at the end of the novel.

Of the responses to evil the runner's is the only one to join actively on the side of good. Once again we must remind ourselves that *A Fable* is only incidentally about war, that it is primarily about man and the ideal way of adjusting to the problems of existence. From the old Negro the runner learns that "Evil is a part of man, evil and sin and cowardice, the

18 *Ibid.*, 75.   19 *Ibid.*, 210.   20 *Ibid.*, 321.

same as repentance and being brave. You got to believe in all of them, or believe in none of them. Believe that man is capable of all of them, or he aint capable of none."[21] And the runner perceives his deficiency. " 'Thanks,' the runner said. 'Maybe what I need is to have to meet somebody. To believe. Not in anything: just to believe.' "[22] As a consequence he acts, but his act is merely a corollary, an attendant circumstance in this situation. The important thing is that he should believe. He alone, of the three who discover evil, regains faith.

v

Another aspect of Faulkner's comment on the human situation and the nature of evil is provided by the old general and the corporal and their relationship. The old general, symbol of God, is the father of the corporal, symbol of Christ. On Thursday night, the night before the "crucifixion," the father takes the son onto the "mount" to test him. The scene recalls in combination three separate occasions in the New Testament: the temptation of Christ in the desert, the Sermon on the Mount, and The Agony in the Garden. To understand the full significance of this scene, it is necessary to remind ourselves that Christ is the son of man as well as of God. The two are in fact the same. As the son of man, He is man advanced to the godly state—man with the evil and weakness eradicated.

The general first tempts his son with liberty and power. He will give him his car, complete with pennant, by means of which he can travel anywhere in Allied Europe. He offers to transfer his worldly power, now the greatest on earth, to its natural inheritor. The corporal refuses to desert those who trust in him. The general reminds him that, on the contrary,

21 *Ibid.*, 203.
22 *Ibid.*, 203.

they have deserted him. He is answered by the reminder that there are still ten who are faithful. It is clear, however, that there need be only one with faith in order to give validity to the martyrdom. The final temptation is the most difficult to resist. It is the opportunity to live. But this is also rejected by the corporal. He is aware that to fulfill his destiny and to give validity to his action of a few days before he must sacrifice his life, and by doing so demonstrate the irreconcilability of the issues of the struggle he has begun. At stake in this exchange with the general is the corporal's belief in man's fundamental goodness. He asserts that man will endure; ironically enough the general agrees with him. In fact, the father goes further in humanistic affirmation than the son; he asserts that man will prevail. On this note they descend from the "mount."

This final agreement can be explained in only one way. One must understand the ironic duality of the character of the general. He is both God and the devil. He is the father of man, literally, and has the accompanying sense of love, and he is the tempter of man. Man has, so to speak, two fathers. Throughout the novel the old general has been shown as a figure of limitless power. As I have demonstrated before, however, he never assumes responsibility; he always gives man the choice. The old general merely accedes to the wish of the corporal to die and to the cry of the people for a death. In this he parallels Pontius Pilate, who also washed his hands of responsibility. If man chooses him to act as the devil, he fills that role, but as he admits in his last interview with the Norman, he would be equally pliable to the wishes of man if man were to choose uniformly in favor of goodness. Polchek, the betrayer, has indicated that man will not at present so choose. The son of man has been betrayed.

That the old general is discontent with man's present choice is clear throughout. His compliance with man's wishes does not prevent his suffering at what man forces him to do. He is first described as one who "no longer believed in anything but his *disillusion* and his intelligence and his limitless power."[23] (Italics are mine.) His own point of view is again represented when he explains the crucifixion to the Norman:

> If he does, if he accepts his life, keeps his life, he will have abrogated his own gesture and martyrdom. If I gave him his life tonight, I myself could render null and void what you call the hope and the dream of his sacrifice. By destroying his life tomorrow morning, I will establish forever that he didn't even live in vain, let alone die so. Now tell me who's afraid?[24]

Finally he makes the comment that, as we have seen, demonstrates his basic sympathy with Christ's outlook: " 'They will do more,' the old general said proudly. 'They will prevail.' "[25] Apparently the disillusion which characterized him early in the novel has been replaced, because of the corporal's act, by a restoration of faith in man. He is naturally proud of man, who is the product of his own creation.

I have shown the general as part of a scheme in which he has a pliable role, and it is perhaps necessary to emphasize this reading in opposition to those who claim that the general is all devil. In his interview with the corporal, he says:

> I champion of this mundane earth which, whether I like it or not, is, and to which I did not ask to come, yet since I am here, not only must stop but intend to stop during my alotted while; you champion of an esoteric realm of man's baseless hopes and his infinite capacity—no: passion—for unfact.[26]

This account of himself is, however, only one of those possible.

[23] *Ibid.*, 13.
[24] *Ibid.*, 332.
[25] *Ibid.*, 354.
[26] *Ibid.*, 348.

He is offering that view of himself which man on the whole has chosen as opposed to the other possible view represented by Christ. In his opposition to his own son, he stands, like Pilate, as the people's representative. He therefore pictures himself in the role thrust upon him. His other potential role is sufficiently indicated by the evidence presented above.

Since the corporal represents the ideal for man, the nature of his character and conduct is of obvious importance for the meaning of the novel. The corporal emphasizes the human aspects of the New Testament God rather than His supernatural characteristics. The miracles he performs are here exemplary acts of humanitarianism. We learn that on one occasion he organized a collection to provide money so that a blind girl could undergo surgery. On another occasion he turned a dice game into a wedding celebration, using the stake money for the provision of wine. These are his miracles. And the corporal is the Christ of peace.[27] He is the man who forgives all sinners, whose faith resides in man. He is the Christ described by the old porter who has lost his son in the war. The resurrection he will effect for the world is to restore to them the life they already have and would have lost.

> "Pah," the old man said; it sounded almost like spitting. "What does it matter, whether or not He brings my son back with Him? My son, or yours, or any other man's? *My* son? Even the whole million of them we have lost since that day four years ago, the billion since that day eighteen hundred and eighty-five years ago. The ones He will restore to life are the ones that would have died since eight o'clock this morning."[28]

[27] Faulkner's personification of abstract concepts found in the New Testament can often be traced to specific pronouncements, as in this case: "Blessed are the peace makers; for they shall be called the children of God." Matt. 5 : 9.

[28] *A Fable*, 81; "God is not the God of the dead, but of the living," Matt. 22 : 32.

vi

Allegorically, the characters of *A Fable* represent fragmented aspects of a whole. The meaning of the novel emerges from the dynamic conflict of the two sides of man personified in this way: Christ is one half of man betrayed by his other half, Judas-Polchek. As Faulkner sees it, however, the battle is unequal. The right man knows he is right; the wrong is plagued by a sense of guilt. In the same way the right side finds it easier to overcome the evil. The corporal believes in the ability of man to lead a selfless, humanistic existence. This faith is not shaken by the knowledge of his betrayal, which merely indicates that at present man is still divided. Man, not yet an integrated entity, still betrays himself.

Ranged against this faith in man is the military outlook which denies man any faculty for responsibility. This attitude is expressed by Lallemont when he paints a picture of man as an irresponsible, herdlike mass, incapable of direction save when a Carlylean strong man "with his sword for paddle . . . heaps and pounds and stiffens the malleable mass."[29] These are the two antithetical views of man that pervade the novel and provide its meaning. There is, however, a more obvious antithesis—the corporal and war. The German general blames the politicians for the war; Gragnon blames an abstract "war," without examining its origin; the men blame the officers, and the officers blame the men; the people blame the enemy. Within the war system we are shown that the very armies bent on destroying each other can momentarily collaborate to crush the one man who seeks and attains peace, which is of course ironically the very subject, object, and cause of the war. This over-all picture of wild self-destruction and senseless misalliance is a presentation of chaos. Faulkner has said that God represents harmony. What he means by this, I believe, is

[29] *A Fable*, 30.

that the universe, and man especially is driven by some sort of inexplicable divine principle towards harmony, towards oneness. Love, then, would be a divine attribute. In other words, what Faulkner means by God is in *A Fable* allegorically presented as Christ, or this principle given human embodiment. The God-figure of the people is not the real God at all, but an ironic parody of the traditional orthodox God, a kind of Blakian "Nobodaddy" that is really a projection of human fears and desires. I am reminded most strongly of Shelley's "Prometheus Unbound," where a similar allegory is more precisely presented. There Jove is such a God, seeming to have a power which is not really his. Only Prometheus recognizes this fact and thus comes to have a controlling power over Jove himself, who is a false God and dependent on man. The corporal, or Faulkner's Christ, is then more Promethian in a Shelleyan sense than anything else. The corporal is the first individual described in the novel to have appraised the situation in which he finds himself and to have acted upon his conviction that such a situation should and could be changed. This is the paradigm of behavior for all men. Chaos may be overcome by judging one's situation according to a fixed set of humanist values.

The need for such a fixed scale of values is demonstrated time and again in Faulkner's work and in several instances in *A Fable*. Some men have an unfortunate past and an undesirable environment which they are helpless to change. Gragnon is a case in point. He had had a loveless past; he had failed to achieve a union with other people:

> [He remembers] the solitude which was his origin and his ancestry and his birthright, the Sisters—the Father himself when he would arrive with his inconsolable dedicated eyes and his hands gentle enough but sonless, which had never caressed nor struck in anger and love and fear and hope and pride, boy's flesh

sprung from his flesh and bearing his immortality in the same intolerant love and hope and pride, wiser perhaps than the Sisters were, less tender than they were tender, but no less compassionate, knowing nothing as the Sisters knew nothing too—saying: "The Mother of Christ, the Mother of all, is your mother"; not enough because he didn't want the mother of all nor the mother of Christ either: he wanted the mother of One.[30]

When it is time to grieve Gragnon is incapable of experiencing normal and desirable human responses—he cannot cry. Because of his past he is unable to comprehend men—his own soldiers, for instance. He believes that they mutinied out of hatred for him. His deficiency as a man, let us call it his immaturity, is underlined by his failure to understand his former aide. The latter tries to tell him what courage is: "Yes. Courage. When you stop to pity, the world runs over you. It takes pride to be that brave."[31] He then demonstrates his own courage by selflessly giving his life. But Gragnon never does fully comprehend that kind of bravery.

Faulkner customarily explains men by showing their past. Another soldier, an American, is briefly described in this way:

> His name was Buchwald. His grandfather had been rabbi of a Minsk synagogue until a Cossack sergeant beat his brains out with the shod hooves of a horse. His father was a tailor; he himself was born on the fourth floor of a walk-up, cold-water Brooklyn tenement.[32]

When Faulkner draws such pictures, he does so to indicate to the reader the result of an absence of values which are outside of, and unaffected by, individual circumstances. Such values have validity because of their basis in those characteristics fundamental to all men at all times in all places.

[30] *Ibid.*, 42.
[31] *Ibid.*, 45.
[32] *Ibid.*, 372.

The portrayal of Christ in *A Fable* is an ironic rationalization of the New Testament from the conception to the resurrection. The ideal man is he who can shape his own destiny by accepting responsibility for his state and choosing between good and evil. This humanistic interpretation of the New Testament leads to a criticism of those who quote the Good Book, but fail to live the spirit of Christianity. Such criticism is found in many of Faulkner's writings. In *A Fable* a Catholic priest bears the brunt of Faulkner's disdain. On the night before the crucifixion a priest comes to the corporal to persuade him to refuse martyrdom. The priest quotes from the Bible. The corporal cannot read. But the illiterate corporal becomes the object of supplication from the learned priest. The priest is without real faith; he is a cynic, finding himself involved in an inescapable net of dogma, affirmations, denials, and explanations.

> "Then I'll cite for you, plead for you," the priest said. "It wasn't He with his humility and pity and sacrifice that converted the world; it was pagan and bloody Rome which did it with His martyrdom; furious and intractable dreamers had been bringing that same dream out of Asia Minor for three hundred years until at last one found a caesar foolish enough to crucify him."[33]

And again:

> Because He even said it Himself: *On this rock I found My church*, even while He didn't—and never would—realise the true significance of what He was saying, believing still that He was speaking poetic metaphor, synonym, parable—that *rock* meant unstable inconstant heart, and *church* meant airy faith.[34]

He ends by committing suicide, unable to live with the truth, unprepared to do so, and unable to admit his own cynicism.

[33] *Ibid.*, 363.
[34] *Ibid.*, 364.

For him, Christ cannot be outside the church, simple faith cannot be enough.

Faulkner's answer to man's predicament comprises a type of nonformal Christianity. Love of man is the basis of it. All men must live by the same values. Christ is really a humanitarian everyman.

vii

When the runner says that he needs to believe "Not in anything: just to believe,"[35] he provides the clue to the weakness of *A Fable*. In *Requiem for a Nun*, Faulkner has Nancy Mannigoe give the same advice to Temple Stevens. The runner has "clarified" the hollowness of this "philosophy." In the earlier novel we could at least speculate on various objects for the imperative "Believe!" but now the inadequacy of Faulkner's didacticism is painfully obvious.

The strength of the portrait of Dilsey in *The Sound and the Fury* comes partly from Faulkner's refusal to explain her inexplicable faith in the Christian absolute. Forced by the pressure of renown to make his own faith clearer, Faulkner has revealed his inability to do so. It is one thing to assert that a belief in Christian values leads to the "good life," but quite another to try to explain the process leading to such faith. The attempt to do so leads to artistic failure. As it is, he is in this work a victim of his own naïveté.

Faulkner fails in this novel because he tries to take a rational approach to the irrational, the mythical. Although individual episodes become striking metaphors to explain in general terms the need for human love and involvement, the entire novel suffers from an unwieldly series of repetitions. One such metaphor is enough! Faulkner appears to have tried to explain to himself the validity of humanism as a Godless religion and to have come back to his asserted starting point.

[35] *Ibid.*, 203.

A *Fable* has many faults as a result of its didactic impulse. Any reader would have much justification for rejecting it as entertaining reading matter. It is characterized by absence of dialogue, tortuous syntax, and long sententious monologues. In much of his earlier work, in the attempt to portray highly complex human emotions, Faulkner obliged his characters by interpreting their thoughts with his own linguistic equipment. In this way he succeeded in portraying their feelings without sacrificing the reader's conception of the character. For instance, consider the description of Joe Christmas' reflections on his sexual relationship to Joanna Burden:

> Sometimes he thought of it in that way, remembering the hard, untearful and unselfpitying and almost manlike yielding of that surrender. A spiritual privacy so long intact that its own instinct for preservation had immolated it, its physical phase the strength and fortitude of a man. A dual personality: the one the woman at first sight of whom in the lifted candle (or perhaps the very sound of the slippered approaching feet) there had opened before him, instantaneous as a landscape in a lightningflash, a horizon of physical security and adultery if not pleasure; the other the mantrained muscles and the mantrained habit of thinking born of heritage and environment with which he had to fight up to the final instant. There was no feminine vacillation, no coyness of obvious desire and intention to succumb at last. It was as if he struggled physically with another man for an object of no actual value to either, and for which they struggled on principle alone.[36]

In *A Fable*, on the other hand, Faulkner seems content to disregard his characters as people, making no pretense at realization or illusion, using them merely as unlikely mouthpieces. Here are the words of Martha, the uneducated, probably illiterate farm girl, as she indicts the old general:

> Oh you were generous; nobody denied that. Because how

[36] *Light in August*, 221-22.

could you have known that the money which was to have bought you immunity from the consequence of your youthful folly—a dowry if the child should be a girl, a tilted scrap of pasture and a flock to graze it if a boy, and a wife for him in time and so even the same grandchildren to immobilise your folly's partner forever beyond the geographic range of your vulnerability—would instead accomplish the exact opposite by paying our passage to Beirut and—with what was left over—becoming what was its original intent: a dowry?[37]

Another example of Faulkner's indifference to the needs of fiction is found in the meeting of the Norman with the old general in the desert. The Norman has sought out his idol and upon seeing him, makes a long speech that begins in this way:

I know. They thought you were hiding. They were afraid of you at first. Then they decided you were just a fool who insisted on becoming a marshal of France at fifty instead of forty-five, using the power and influence at twenty-one and -two and -three and -four and -five to evade at forty-five the baton you would have nothing left to fend off at fifty; the power and the influence to escape the power and influence, the world to escape the world; to free yourself of flesh without having to die, without having to lose the awareness that you were free of flesh: not to escape from it and you could not be immune to it nor did you want to be: only to be free of it, to be conscious always that you were merely at armistice with it at the price of constant and unflagging vigilance, because without that consciousness, flesh would not exist for you to be free of it and so there would be nothing anywhere for you to be free of. Oh yes, I knew: the English poet Byron's dream or wish or cry that all living women had but one single mouth for his kiss: the supreme golden youth who encompassed all flesh by putting, still virgin to it, all flesh away. But I knew better: who sought a desert not as Simeon did but as Anthony, using Mithridates and Heliogabalus not merely to

[37] A Fable, 29.

acquire a roosting-place for contempt and scorn, but for fee to the cave where the lion itself lay down: who—the ones who feared you once—believed that they had seen ambition and greed themselves default before one seventeen-year-old child—had seen the whole vast hitherto invulnerable hegemony of ruthlessness and rapacity reveal itself unfearsome and hollow when even that uncle and that godfather could not cope with your crime or defalcation, as though so poor and thin was the ambition and greed to which even that uncle and that godfather were dedicant, that voracity itself had repudiated them who had been its primest pillars and its supremest crown and glory.[38]

My complaint is not merely about the language itself; it is that the Norman is speaking only out of a need to express something to himself, yet he is not Hamlet alone on a stage. He *is* greeting another person. The writer must surely meet his obligation to take into account the circumstances in which he himself has placed his characters.

Putting the characters of the novels aside, Faulkner's own description often reaches a symbolic minuteness that is extremely irritating, as in the following illustration:

So the aide was flanking, not the division commander but the chief-of-staff, pacing him correctly on the left, back to the open door beyond which the provost officer waited while the division commander passed through it.

Whereupon the aide not only effaced from the room the entire significance of the surrendered sabre, he obliterated from it the whole gauche inference of war. As he stepped quickly and lightly and even a little swaggeringly toward the open door beyond which the division commander and the provost officer had vanished, it was as though, in declining in advance to hold the door for the division commander (even though the division commander had already declined the courtesy in advance by not waiting for it), he had not merely retaliated upon the junior

[38] *Ibid.*, 258–59.

general for the junior's affrontment to the senior general's prece-
dence, he had used the junior as the instrument to postulate both
himself and the chief-of-staff as being irrevocably alien and invincibly unconcerned with everything the room and those contained represented—the very tall elegantly thin captain of twenty-
eight or thirty with the face and body of a durable matinee idol,
who might have been a creature from another planet, anachron-
istic and immune, inviolable, so invincibly homeless as to be completely and impregnably at home on this or any other planet
where he might find himself: not even of tomorrow but of the day
before it, projected by reverse avatar back into a world where
what remained of lost and finished man struggled feebly for a
moment yet among the jumbled ruins of his yesterdays—a creature
who had survived intact the fact that he had no place, no business
whatever, in war, who for all gain or loss to war's inexorable
gambit or that of the frantic crumbling nations either, might as
well have been floating gowned and capped (and with the
golden tassel of a lordship too, since he looked more like a scion
than any duke's son) across an Oxford or Cambridge quadrangle,
compelling those watching him and the chief-of-staff to condone
the deodorization of war's effluvium even from the uniforms they
wore, leaving them simply costumes, stepping rapidly and lightly
and elegantly past the chief-of-staff to grasp the knob and shut
the door until the latch caught, then turned the knob and opened
the door and clicked not to attention but into a rigid brief inclina-
tion from the waist as the chief-of-staff passed through it.[39]

Here the language does just the opposite of what it is ideally
supposed to do: it sets up a barrier between the intention of
the words and the reader. One becomes too conscious of the
words themselves. Contrast the following description from
Absalom, Absalom!:

Quentin and Shreve stared at one another—glared rather—their
quiet regular breathing vaporizing faintly and steadily in the now
[39] *Ibid.*, 234–35.

tomblike air. There was something curious in the way they looked at one another, curious and quiet and profoundly intent, not at all as two young men might look at each other but almost as a youth and a very young girl might out of virginity itself—a sort of hushed and naked searching, each looked burdened with youth's immemorial obsession not with time's dragging weight which the old live with but with its fluidity: the bright heels of all the lost moments of fifteen and sixteen.[40]

There is no single descriptive paragraph as effective and eloquent as that in all the many pages of *A Fable*.

In the events of the novel we find the same disregard of the artistic concerns to which Faulkner so obviously attends in most of his earlier work. The main action of the novel is interrupted for the purpose of introducing scenes which make no contribution to the narrative development of the novel and are obviously and crudely incorporated to provide further static commentary on an already elaborate allegory. An example of this is the recognition scene wherein the corporal is identified by a British and an American officer as a man whom they both knew at different times to have died. The ever-presence of Christ, his continual resurrection, is clearly being pointed up here, yet Faulkner must feel that he has failed to emphasize his meaning symbolically in the normal narrative course of the novel and that he must, therefore, clarify his meaning with such redundant scenes.

Similarly, the horse-racing episode is dragged into the novel on the flimsiest of pretexts. Admirable in itself, it can be connected with the rest of the novel only by a powerful imaginative effort on the part of the reader. As an allegory on the death of religion and the predominance of material values, it is effective, but its failure to become an integral part of *A Fable* is lamentable. It would seem here that the urgency of

[40] *Absalom, Absalom!*, 299.

the message has moved Faulkner away from the realism and the dramatic power that often characterized his earlier work. The whole emphasis of this Christ fable is clearly sermon-like. The sententious tone of the entire novel is didactic and cannot be mistaken for anything but the presentation of a moral viewpoint. Instead of the ideas growing out of the very framework of the house of fiction, the structure has been imposed upon a preconceived thesis, and the novel is contrived in the service of a point of view.

There is a considerable difference, for example, between Benjamin Compson, Joe Christmas, and the corporal. Yet each of these characters in some way represents Christ. Benjy is a highly wrought portrayal of an idiot serving a dramatically integral function in *The Sound and the Fury*; Christmas is a Southerner of dubious racial origin searching desperately for his moral identity. They are these things before they are anything else. The corporal, on the other hand, is not a corporal first—he is in no way a fully realized character; he is merely a morality figure, the embodiment of an idea. When Vivian Mercier says that the horse episode "symbolizes the human qualities that Faulkner wishes to celebrate better than do all his attempts to recreate, in humanistic terms, the symbols of the Gospels, which must, for Christians, in the last analysis embody a superhuman reality," he means that Faulkner is more convincing as a novelist than as a preacher.[41] He is effective only when his characters emerge from his imagination; he fails when they are laboriously pieced together out of his rationale. Maxwell Geismar is mistaken, however, when he asserts, "But a quarter of a century ago (1929) Faulkner was not concerned with upholding the old verities he lauded in the Nobel Prize address. His purpose then was to show the

[41] "Search for Universality That Led Too Far from Home," *Commonweal*, Vol. LX (August 6, 1954), 444.

life around him."[42] Faulkner never was merely concerned with showing the life around him. He has always provided a commentary on that life. His comments have always been the same. In the past, however, many (including Mr. Geismar) were tricked into reading Faulkner's works merely as vivid pictures of Southern life and history; tricked by the infinite skill with which the author controlled meaning and symbol, providing the levels of meaning which, parable-fashion, characterize all great literature. In *A Fable* no new point of view is present. What was once submerged has surfaced for all to see.

[42] "A Fable," *American Moderns, from Rebellion to Conformity* (New York, 1958), 99.

CHAPTER VII

The Town
"All people learn a little more"

The *Town* is an extension and elaboration of *The Hamlet*, different in technique but almost identical in meaning. The ambitions of the Snopeses are further recorded here, and Flem continues his climb towards those empty goals which he sees are the dreams and hopes of all those around him—money and power, and to get them and keep them, respectability. Flem is able to succeed because of the faults in Jefferson, just as he was able to succeed earlier because of the faults in Frenchman's Bend.[1] In the town the principal concern is for "civic virtue." One of the finest passages in *The Town*, central to its meaning, is this metaphorical description of evil and society's reaction to it:

> It dont go away; it just stops being so glaring in sight, barked over; there is a lump, a bump of course, but after a while the other trees forgive that and everything else accepts that tree and that bump too until one day the saw or the axe goes into it and hits that old nail.[2]

Like many other writers, Faulkner is suggesting that evil does not ever disappear—it is merely temporarily out of sight—but one way or another it turns up again and plays some part in whatever shape the future takes. The people of Jefferson want only to cover up and hide from sight the evil in their

[1] I have pursued this idea of the moral weaknesses inherent in Frenchman's Bend in "The 'Normality' of Snopesism: Universal Themes in Faulkner's *The Hamlet*," *Wisconsin Studies*, Vol. III (Winter, 1962), 25–34.

[2] *The Town* (New York, 1957), 303.

midst. To fight Snopesism would involve examining and then changing themselves first, and rather than make the effort, undergo the strain, they will absorb Snopeses and Snopesism, demanding only that it conform to their own pattern of evil and appear respectable.

Even more pointedly here does Flem remind us of Sutpen. He needs the big house and the name. By the end of the novel we find that he has "to go and watch how the carpenters was getting along with his new house (it was going to have colyums across the front now, I mean the extry big ones so even a feller that never seen colyums before wouldn't have no doubt a-tall what they was . . . ."[3] Flem assumes all the activities most valued in Jefferson. He meets the standards set by the "God-fearing upright embattled Christian Jeffersons and Yoknapatawphas too that can proudly affirm that never in their life did they ever have one minute's fun that the most innocent little child couldn't a stood right there and watched."[4] What differentiates Flem from his neighbors in Jefferson is the absence of conscience, of guilt, of suffering. He is in the realm of social behavior and economic values what McEachern of *Light in August* is in the realm of religion: both have falsely extracted from their codes the word without the spirit, each has mistaken appearance for reality, like collectors of emptied bird eggs. Both are incorporated in the fiction to reveal the latent dangers in the societies which they exploit. We are urged to see the difference between them and their models because the hope for Jeffersonians and everybody else is to concentrate on the differences and not on the similarities of Flem and his fellow money-grabbers. It is in the consultation of conscience and the examination of values and motives that men become human, and it is for this reason that Flem never does appear to be human. No doubt, no anguish, no re-

---

[3] *Ibid.*, 352.   [4] *Ibid.*, 350.

gret ever occurs to him, but like a computing machine he only figures, reckoning all the information to come up with an answer that will provide a profit or loss in purely financial terms. The works of the Snopes Trilogy are all basically satirical. Flem is an exaggerated parody of the society in which he lives, and like all satirical figures, Flem is his author's scapegoat, bearing the burden of all the faults and dangers that Faulkner sees as inherent in the society which nurtured him. Only Mrs. Armstid and Wallstreet Snopes are never exploited by Flem and therefore never defeated by him, because they will not enter the contest under his rules; to escape Flem is to defeat him since he lives like a parasite on those who will "succour" him and his vices; to live by another set of rules is to isolate him, to leave him competitorless in his ruthless game, to brush him out from his warm comfortable fold in the skin.

There is much comment in *The Town* on formal religion in Jefferson, and, as we would expect, it is of the most critical kind. Lip service and superficial piety have failed to protect Jefferson from Snopes. Faulkner tells us that "the very fabric of Baptist and Methodist life is delusion, nothing."[5] The only answer to Flem is to live with complete honesty, dignity, and humanity. Manfred De Spain, the mayor of the town, its elected symbol and representative, is the first to assist Flem by pursuing Eula and making her his mistress. Let us look at this a little more closely. It is true that Manfred is rendering Eula a service, playing a part which the impotent Flem (we later find out) cannot play and only doing what every other male in Jefferson wanted to do. We do not condemn him, nor does Faulkner, for loving Eula. We do condemn him, however, for the kind of price he pays. He bribes Flem to let him use his wife, and Flem is only too happy to use his wife for his own advancement. Manfred wants to be the gallant adulterer and

5 *Ibid.*, 308.

the respectable mayor, and his success is at the price of providing Flem an unshakable foothold in the town. In other words, it is the hidden corruption, the deception, the hypocrisy which aids Flem, not the evil but the hiding it, or the attempt to hide it. While the cracks in the wall are being feverishly papered over, the whole edifice is disintegrating. De Spain's father found himself in bitter conflict with Ab Snopes. Ironically, his son aids and abets Ab's son. De Spain, by yielding to his own promiscuity, puts himself into Flem's hands. Stevens fails to prevent the affair because he, too, lends a hand with the papering even while trying to reach behind and plaster the cracks, but he is unable to accomplish this gymnastic feat.

In the case of Montgomery Ward Snopes, Stevens hides the truth once more, and Flem is able to exploit both his and the community's insistence on respectable appearances at the expense of truth. Stevens, like the rest, is more concerned with respectability than virtue, and he permits Flem to change the charge of pornography-peddling to whisky-selling. When Montgomery Ward Snopes came back from France, he brought with him some pornographic slides or photographs which became the basis for a profitable business. Under cover of a photography studio this particular Snopes gives a show nightly and is never short of male customers. Here again the corruption of the town itself is necessary to the the success of the Snopes enterprise. Significantly, Snopes is able to corrupt the law itself on all its levels: first, Grover Cleveland Winbush, the night marshal, who actually belongs to the photography club; then Hub Hampton, the very sheriff who arrests Snopes on a trumped-up charge, but who knows the truth; and finally, Gavin Stevens himself, county attorney, who permits the original charge to be changed to bootlegging and does so for the same reason as Flem, the desire for respectability.

The case of I. O. Snopes provides a similar instance. I. O. has been making a practice of buying mules and employing Mr. Hait to take them near enough to the railroad line and keep them tied there until a train kills them. On Mr. Hait's last trip he manages to get himself killed, whereupon I. O.'s business disappears and Mrs. Hait receives a large sum of money in railroad compensation. The early story "Mule in the Yard" is here incorporated, one of the events of which now leads to a mishap, and Mrs. Hait's house burns down. Before a major legal conflict between Mrs. Hait and I. O., whose mules were in her yard, can occur, in steps Flem again and gives Mrs. Hait the deed to her house, mortgaged previously at his bank, and pays I. O. for the mules which were killed on the last railroad trip on the condition that I. O. go to Frenchman's Bend and never return to Jefferson. Significantly, the paid witness to Flem's transactions is Gavin Stevens, who is mistakenly rather pleased with the way it has turned out and is only too happy, once again, to accept the comfortable compromise that Flem has designed. The next day, however, it is Ratliff who sees the implications and says of them to Gavin's nephew, Charles, "Because soon as you set down to laugh at it, you find out it aint funny a-tall."[6] He continues to explain why Flem's actions are terrifying:

> When it's jest money and power a man wants, there is usually some place where he will stop; there's always one thing at least that ever—every man wont do for jest money. But when it's respectability he finds out he wants and has got to have, there aint nothing he wont do to get it and then keep it.[7]

Since *The Hamlet*, Ratliff has learned that there is nothing to be gained by trying to oppose Flem personally. In this novel he remains aloof from all direct dealings with Flem and in-

---

[6] *Ibid.*, 257.   [7] *Ibid.*, 259.

stead joins with Wall Snopes in the honest enterprise of providing groceries at reasonable prices. The rather crudely expressed moral of this part of *The Town* is that Wall and Ratliff, by remaining perfectly honest and permitting no cupboard skeletons, are able to remain perfectly independent of Flem and his kind; Flem can have no hold over generous and honest men.

If there was any doubt before the publication of *The Town* that Snopes is a parody of everyman at his weakest, there should be none now. Eck is a Snopes, and he breaks his neck saving the life, not only of another man but of a Negro. He finally loses his life needlessly looking for a little boy thought to be lost. His son, Wallstreet, works hard and honestly, rising through his own industry and the principle of working for a small profit margin. These are good Snopeses, but there is also mention of a bad non-Snopes that is equally revealing: "Wilbur Provine lived in Frenchman's Bend too. Ratliff said he was really a Snopes; that when Providence realised that Eck Snopes was going to fail his lineage and tradition, it hunted around quick and produced Wilbur Provine to plug the gap."[8] Flem has his allies and enemies, both inside and outside the family. It is Ratliff who has to explain to Stevens that Snopes is not a name but a condition:

> "Yes," I said. "I've heard about that. I wonder why she never changed their name."
> "No, no," he said. "You dont understand. She dont want to change it. She jest wants to live it down. She aint trying to drag him by the hair out of Snopes, to escape from Snopes. She's got to purify Snopes itself. She's got to beat Snopes from the inside."[9]

You can beat Snopes "from the inside" or not at all.

Flem is helped to prominence by civic concern for externals,

8 *Ibid.*, 168.   9 *Ibid.*, 149–50.

a hypocritical insistence on keeping up appearances and a failure to insist on the truth, on purification at the expense of momentary pain. There are only two brief indications in the novel of successful opposition to Flem. One of them we have already seen in Eck and Wall. The other is illustrated by the conduct of two Negroes, Tom Tom and Tomey's Turl. Brought into opposition by Flem and among his earliest Jefferson victims, they find that Snopesism is a mutual enemy. Their only hope is therefore in mutual trust and co-operation. As long as they deceive each other (Turl is sleeping regularly with Tom Tom's wife), Flem can use them. They discover that "Tom Tom's home violated not by Tomey's Turl but by Flem Snopes; Turl's life and limbs put into frantic jeopardy not by Tom Tom but by Flem Snopes."[10] They confront each other and come to an understanding and a realization of their own past naïveté. As a result, Flem loses his stolen brass. The incident occurs early in the novel. It is a comment on the defeat of Flem through harmony; in contrast to this, all that follows reveals Flem's rise because of social divisiveness.

If we survey Flem's career we will see that every success is due to some existing weakness in the social system. His first job and his hold over the Varners, his marriage, his pony auction, his acquisition of the Jefferson restaurant, his rise to superintendent of the power plant, and then to the presidency of the bank, all are directly traceable to the faults and errors and weaknesses of others. The existing system of values is empty and pointless.

Eula becomes a kind of sacrificial figure in the power struggle for money and respectability. She is first sacrificed to Flem by her parents, especially Will Varner, who insists on respectability at all costs and must find a father for Eula's coming illegitimate child. This is not easy to do in the Puritan hamlet,

10 *Ibid.*, 28.

and only Flem is willing to exploit the situation. Later Eula
is sacrificed by Flem to Manfred, who is willing to accept the
sacrifice at any cost, even at the cost of the community which
he is supposed to serve. Gavin becomes her futile champion.
She finally makes a last gesture of rejection and relinquishment when she commits suicide. Eula is capable of love, of
giving and accepting real love (characterized by selflessness),
but in her world she can find none.

> "She was bored. She loved, had a capacity to love, for love, to
> give and accept love. Only she tried twice and failed twice to find
> somebody not just strong enough to deserve, earn it, match it,
> but even brave enough to accept it. Yes," he [Gavin] said, sitting
> there crying, not even trying to hide his face from us, "of course
> she was bored."[11]

It takes real courage to love. There is very little courage in
Jefferson.

The "love" that remains in modern Jefferson is represented
mechanically, "the sole single manifestation which love or
anyway desire was capable of assuming in Jefferson, was
rushing slow past the specific house with the cut-out wide
open."[12] This is Faulkner's bitter comment on a world where
human values have been reduced to mechanical form, where
machines have displaced men, because men were incapable
or unwilling to accept the challenges of life.

The final portrait of Snopesism in *The Town* is the most horrific of all. It seems that the source of horror is most readily
found in a total inversion of what is normally beneficent. The
child become monster is probably as terrifying a concept as
any, so fixed is our assurance of the innocence and trust and
love of children. The last generation of Snopes is not human
at all, let alone childlike:

11 *Ibid.*, 359.
12 *Ibid.*, 196.

. . . they didn't look like children; if there was one thing in the world they didn't look like it was children, with kind of dark pasty faces and black hair that looked like somebody had put a bowl on top of their heads and then cut their hair up to the rim of the bowl with a dull knife, and perfectly black perfectly still eyes that nobody in Jefferson (Yoknapatawpha County either) ever afterward claimed they saw blink.[13]

They are the "four things" that get off the train in Jefferson. It is Flem, of course, that sends them out of Jefferson, but not before their presence has registered as a prophecy on the future of the race. Just as the memory of Jim Bond haunts Quentin in *Absalom, Absalom!*, so these mechanical figures haunt the reader. Born of a combination of Snopes and Indian, they represent the conclusion of the American experiment, a total misuse of all the promise latent in the New World. Rapacity and the service of abstraction lead to dehumanization. Flem is only a stage in a process—he is merely one aspect of man's degeneration.

In order to root out Snopesism, it is necessary to revert to a different system of values. A complete and honest self-examination is required. Flem can, and does, become a deacon in the Baptist church, but this is a commentary on the church, not on Flem. One of the characters in *The Town* can view the presence of Snopeses as a privilege, and rightly so:

. . . we got them now; they're ourn now; I dont know jest what Jefferson could a committed back there whenever it was, to have won this punishment, gained this right, earned this privilege. But we did. So it's for us to cope, to resist; us to endure, and (if we can) survive.[14]

In other words Snopesism is an aspect of man similar to that

13 *Ibid.*, 360.
14 *Ibid.*, 102.

which evolves in Adam after the Fall. This is a symbol of *felix culpa* in Faulkner's work, a privilege of choosing given to man so that he may become more than a "mechanical Adam." It is only after the Fall that God can say, "Behold, the man is become as one of us, to know good and evil." To have the privilege of Snopeses is to have the privilege of choosing, of making the far-reaching Kantian decision that legislates for all men. The story of Snopeses is the story of man after the Fall. We are always confronted with the opportunity for salvation, and for Faulkner that salvation rests in eradicating the system which engendered the Snopeses. To abolish Snopesism is to live by the heart, to insist on truth, and to lead the selfless kind of existence that all of Faulkner's Christian heroes demonstrate.

Between the publication of *The Hamlet* and *The Town* there was a sad change in Faulkner's technique. As I have tried to indicate, Faulkner's concerns have always been the same. In all the novels man is his own persecutor, the maker of his own destiny. The terms of this destiny may have varied slightly, from Dilsey's convinced Christianity to Ike Snopes's love, the purity of which transcends even the perversion. But the search for terms goes on, and in *The Town*, Faulkner has tried to revert to Yoknapatawpha, to Snopes territory after the disappointment of *A Fable.*

The structure of *The Town* rests on two principal techniques. One is anecdotal. The other is discursive. This, I believe, clearly indicates that on the one hand Faulkner wishes to return to the imaginative power of his early fiction, to return to material with which he feels most comfortable, and that on the other hand Faulkner cannot escape his awareness of the limelight in which he now stands. He knows that now his novels are eagerly awaited, and he feels compelled to make his "message" unmistakable. In *The Town,* the anecdotal material is very effective because it is mostly old material. These early short stories are set in a framework of first person commentary and in the present tense. There is some excellent story material here that is not old, and it, too, is very effective. There has apparently been no diminishing of his talent. But he is still self-conscious enough so that his talent is subverted to a deliberate structural process. His novels no longer sustain for their entirety the force of individual anecdotal episodes as they once did.

In *The Town*, Faulkner tries to recover the technique of shifting points of view that he used so successfully in *As I Lay Dying* and *The Sound and the Fury* and indirectly in other novels like *Absalom, Absalom!* and *Light in August*. In those novels the characters reveal themselves in their special interpretations of events. They are also intimately involved in the complexity of the action. In *The Town*, however, the characters seem remote from the action, standing way off like officers behind the line and offering intellectual assessments of the struggle in the distance which loses its gory detail when viewed from so far away. This has the effect of producing a sense of distance in the reader which is the reverse of that achieved in the earlier novels, where in a real sense the action proceeds inside the minds of the commentators and thus compels the reader ever closer to the center of the action. In *Absalom, Absalom!*, for instance, when Quentin finally shouts out that he does not hate the South, the cries echo all too terribly close to our ears. We, too, become Southerners in the novel, searching for an identity in the South. But *The Town* is not really about Gavin Stevens and Chick Mallison and V. K. Ratliff. Of Chick Mallison and V. K. Ratliff, it is undeniably true that there is almost no intention of involving them in the action except in a peripheral and mechanical way.

In all essential respects they emerge as outsiders watching from a distance, regardless of how much they claim to be intimately concerned and involved. Gavin Stevens, however, is shown as having some unconvincing claims to a supposedly passionate and real part in the action. His actions do reveal his state of mind. He is involved not only in a professional capacity but also in the voluntary role of champion of *The Town*. His role is, he believes, to thwart all the aims and methods of Flem Snopes.

But even Gavin Stevens emerges as something apart from *The Town*. He talks so much, analyzes so much, that it has the effect of removing him from what he himself does. He is rather like a J. Alfred Prufrock who does act but never ceases to be the kind of man who could not act. In other words his actions really bear little relation to the rest of him: Gavin Stevens ought to be like Gail Hightower (he *is* like that in *Intruder in the Dust*) because in *The Town* this is the impression he gives. He *seems* weak and ineffectual even though Faulkner tells us he is not.

Now as I said before, the effect of all this is to force the reader away from the action of the novel. This is, I believe, symptomatic of Faulkner's own intellectual distance from the novel, his detached control. This in itself need not be a bad thing except that Faulkner earlier demonstrated that his enormous talent lay in bringing the reader into the action of the novel, in weaving a complex web of psychological revelations. All Faulkner's earlier characters were actors, not critics.

The Town, however, is a far cry, as artistic achievement, from *The Hamlet*, and must finally be reckoned with that body of work which is marred by intrusive and assertive episode and comment. The dialogue lacks realism, the structure is disconcertingly episodic, and the meaning of *The Hamlet* is here emphasized and elaborated in an unnecessary fashion. What was subtle and restrained has become bare and crude. Where the events of *The Hamlet* are revealed as they occur, thus providing a tension and movement, the events told in *The Town* are all in the past. The characters act as story-tellers, reflecting after the event. The drama of reaction to current event and of psychological response to social inter-action is thus lost.

Gavin Stevens is perhaps most detrimental to the novel. Wherever he appears in Faulkner's work, he destroys fictional illusion, creating about him the atmosphere of the pulpit. One cannot but agree with Chick's comment on his uncle: "It was almost like he was talking to himself, like there wasn't any-body or anything that wished he would stop more than he did."[15] It is almost as though Faulkner wished that he could dispense with Stevens, find some other means to make evalua-tion of the events of his fiction. The compulsion that had been a marked element in Faulkner's work since *Intruder in the Dust* seemed to drive him into sententiousness. There was an impatience with fiction as a social corrective, and this led to the use of Stevens. Stevens, however, is not always a mouth-piece for Faulkner. Rather he is a clue to the earnestness of Faulkner's own social conscience.

There are other weaknesses in *The Town*. Eula in *The Hamlet* is all symbol, like Lion in "The Bear." In *The Town*, however, Faulkner tries, and fails, to make her both real and symbolic, whereupon she loses both qualities. Stevens, too, like the reporter of *Pylon*, is an unconvincing Prufrock, and the analogy is made precise by at least one borrowing from Eliot's poem.[16] The difference between the two Snopes novels

[15] *Ibid.*, 45.
[16] Compare the first passage from *The Town*
. . . the interminable time until a few minutes after half past three filled

indicates the kind of difference that separates the best and worst of Faulkner. Although *The Town* is an attempt to revert to a familiar locale and a time and people that Faulkner knows, it is still weakened by sententious moralizing, a superficial structure, undeveloped character, a contrived sequence of events, and an imposed symbolism.

In *The Town*, as in other Faulkner works, the criticism is pointed and often bitter, but it is made because man is worth improving. Faulkner's Nobel Prize speech does not indicate a radical change from a cosmic pessimism to a religious optimism. It is part of Faulkner's long record of human affirmation which never really concerned itself with the structure of any kind of world except a human one or one in which human beings play a leading role. Like Blake, Faulkner might well seem to believe not in matter but in matter-for-experience. Since man is fundamentally good and capable of love, he must therefore retain his individuality.

with a thousand indecisions which each fierce succeeding harassment would revise.
with these lines from "The Love Song of J. Alfred Prufrock":
Time for you and time for me,
And time yet for a hundred indecisions
And for a hundred visions and revisions . . . .
(T. S. Eliot, *Collected Poems, 1909–1935* [New York, 1936], 12.)

CHAPTER VIII

The Mansion
"To trust in God without depending on Him"

T*he Mansion* deals with the career of Flem Snopes
after he has become president of the bank that used to be
owned by Sartoris, and after he has moved into the mansion
which used to belong to the De Spains. He has thus effectively
taken over two of the major achievements, major symbols
perhaps, of two of the oldest families in Yoknapatawpha
County, the nearest thing to an aristocracy in Faulkner's fictional Mississippi. Significantly enough, when Flem does have
the bank and the mansion, he finds he has nothing. That is to
say that Flem is no more satisfied now, no more alive, no more
interested than he ever was. If anything he is rather more
"dead" than ever before, because now the quest for social
supremacy, the only pursuit that gave any drama and meaning
to his life, is over. This is one of the reasons that he dies, that
he passively awaits the arrival of Mink Snopes and quietly
accepts the death Mink has planned for him, even waiting
while Mink fires a second time, as though to suggest that his
approaching state seems to him no different from the one
which he has apparently decided is not worth saving.

The bank and the mansion, between which Flem finally
travels in prosaic routine, are clearly summary symbols of two
tendencies (or pursuits or values or attitudes) which began
long ago in Jefferson and naturally end in their own absurd
parody, Flem. Snopeses are not new to Yoknapatawpha: they
are as old as Sartoris himself, and they have been associated

with the bank just as long. Nor is the Snopes struggle with
De Spain new. Ab Snopes, fifty years earlier, bitterly resented
the arrogance and power and the big house which De Spain
had managed to build upon a flaccid society, using as his tools
both slavery and his own ruthlessness. Materialism (the
bank) and voracious social conflict (the mansion) have
always been at the heart of Jefferson.

Ironically enough, Flem makes the De Spain mansion even
more impressive than it was, having huge new colonial-style
columns erected, yet inside the house he attempts to recon-
struct a little of the atmosphere of the old country cabin,
having a little wooden shelf nailed to the fire place (by a
Snopes relative) where he can put up his feet. Flem's relationship to the mansion is thus symbolic of all that has happened
to him. Society has shown him what it demands, what it
values: the impressive, phony exterior, the appearance of
wealth and superiority and solidity which "the folks owning
the money he was custodian of would some of them be jealous
a little but all of them, even the jealous ones, would be proud
and all of them would approve."[1] But inside, Flem is the same,
belying the exterior; only now he is more alien than ever,
living in a kind of awful isolation, without even the satisfaction of chewing the tobacco he could once afford, so that in
this new house, Flem is not "at home":

> . . . Flem never even went into them [rooms] except to eat in
> the dining room, except that one room at the back where when he
> wasn't in the bed sleeping he was setting in another swivel chair
> like the one in the bank, with his feet propped against the side
> of the fireplace: not reading, not doing nothing, jest setting with
> his hat on, chewing that same little mouth-sized chunk of air he
> had been chewing ever since he quit tobacco when he finally got

[1] William Faulkner, *The Mansion* (New York, 1959), 154.

to Jefferson and heard about chewing gum and then quit chewing gum too when he found out folks considered the vice-president of a bank rich enough not to have to chew anything.[2]

His only comfort now is to rest his feet on "a little wood ledge, not even painted, nailed to the front of that hand-carved hand-painted Mount Vernon mantlepiece at the exact height for Flem to prop his feet on it."[3]

Flem has in fact satisfied society; he has met its demands and participated in its values, but he has found his life increasingly pointless. This is not to suggest that Flem ever realizes this—he is much too mechanical to enjoy or suffer. But for the reader the implications are made quite clear.

The role of Eula Snopes is taken over in *The Mansion* by Linda Snopes. The story of the mother's suffering and endurance now becomes the story of the daughter's. Linda Snopes is the victim of her father's striving for the abstractions valued so highly by the community, much as Eula was. However, in this case, Gavin Stevens has entered the picture, much earlier in fact in *The Town*, where he began to cultivate Linda by exposing her to some of the finest examples of human aspiration and dreaming and planning in Western culture. Although Linda is forced to stay in Jefferson until after her mother's funeral, she does then escape, strengthened by her long association with Stevens, to undertake to be herself in Greenwich Village. She finds in Barton Kohn, a Jewish sculptor, a further source of strength and self-respect; and after losing her husband and her hearing in the Spanish Civil War, she returns to Jefferson to live in quiet sufferance in her father's house, fighting liberal causes with the means at her disposal.

Gavin's fight for Linda Snopes is a fight against Flem Snopes in that she represents everything that Flem is not:

[2] *Ibid.*, 155–56.
[3] *Ibid.*, 156.

sensuality, love, understanding, idealism, and human commitment. Faulkner here attempts to engage Gavin Stevens in the working of the novel more than ever before, but Gavin does not become any more real and comprehensible than he ever was, partly because it is impossible ever to say what exactly gives him his anguish and partly because he is still such an incorrigible speech-maker. The other Faulkner character of whom Stevens most reminds one in his tormented relationship with women is Horace Benbow of *Sanctuary*. Benbow, however, is revealed as tortured by an unholy, almost traditionally distorted reverence for women coupled with a yearning desire and admiration, much in the style of Quentin Compson.

Faulkner, however, does not want to create another Benbow figure in Stevens, and so he tries to make him virile, competent, and even married. He gives us elaborate kissing sequences between Linda and Gavin and tries to draw a thoroughly frank picture. Nevertheless, Gavin Stevens emerges as bewildered, embarrassed, inept, and unhappy, in spite of all Faulkner's attempts to produce a contrary impression. I believe that Faulkner could not really visualize, and therefore could not realize, the characters that he intellectually wanted to create in Linda and Gavin. Neither of these people can be all the things he wanted them to be and still be imaginable to him, but, significantly, he rejected the demands of his imagination and insisted on producing them to conform to his theoretical plans.

The real power and brilliance of the novel lies in the story of Mink Snopes, who is, I believe, the real reason for the existence of the novel, the rest being so much padding. Mink is a single and thoroughly comprehensible person whom Faulkner understands and conceives of fully and perfectly. He is a "dirt" farmer, a share-cropper, who has never had anything but hardship and trouble and grinding physical labor, and whose life is a long unending struggle against an exacting fate. He sees the world as God-run, looked over by "Ole Master," but also as a place of trial where he must encounter a long series of endurance tests, each one putting an increasingly painful strain on his pride and human dignity. Mink feels that he is caught up helplessly in a series of mistakes over which he has no control; instead of control, though, he has resistance and pride, a code of meeting outside demands while not sacrificing his self-respect, and it is this code that finally leads him to shoot Jack Houston. Houston, too, is proud, which is why he becomes Mink's victim in their deadly struggle over a one-dollar-a-pound fee. Mink maintains that he did not want to shoot Houston, that he would rather Houston had not pushed him to it, but having been placed in an impossible position, he loses his power to choose, fate having chosen for him.[4]

Mink seeks revenge, not because he believes it will do him any good but because he cannot think of not taking it, growing as it does out of the old code that he has inherited. Mink, as his name suggests, is an animal. For this reason he is totally innocent. His actions and responses are instinctive and not calculated. His is the jungle existence, and his code is the jungle code. By the demands of that code he is almost heroic, and if blame rests anywhere, it must be on the society that makes existence intolerable for Mink. Jack Houston, who ought to have known better, is almost solely to blame for his own death. One cannot tease a wild animal and expect not to get bitten. Flem does accept the consequences of his actions

---

[4] As a vividly realized monomaniac, Mink naturally recalls Melville's Ahab, who likewise sees himself as the "lieutenant of the fates," having been selected as a victim of a maliciously contrived set of circumstances. The differences are, of course, too numerous to mention here, but the monomania is more easily comprehended in the comparison.

166

as inevitable and knows much better than Houston what constitutes his opposition in the person of Mink. This is the reason for his duping Mink into trying to escape, which leads to an additional eighteen-year sentence. Flem is under no illusion about Mink's role in the order of the jungle code—he knows that not only will Mink seek to take his life, but that nothing can stop him in his attempt. They are, after all, both Snopeses and should understand each other.

This sense of inevitability, the relentlessness of fate, and the closing circle of an ever turning wheel is very strongly conveyed in the novel in an almost Greek, dramatic way. Faulkner conveys fully the impression of the endless passage of identical seasons, the sowing of cotton and its harvesting, the annual struggle with the land and the weather, the aging of people, the graying of hair, and the fatigue of struggle against the brown backdrop of the never changing land. The cyclic atmosphere is made even more real by the almost incredible faith of Mink in the divine system, which, though hard and full of suffering, is at least consistent. Mink "decides" to believe in God again when he finds too many things have gone against him. He stops a jailbreak attempt to save his own life and then finds that one of the escapees is waiting for his release in order to kill him. The warden refuses to release Mink under these circumstances, and so Mink decides to believe in God again in order to get His assistance. Sure enough, the escaped prisoner is killed when a church falls on him in San Diego, California. Now, Mink can get his release. The sense of arbitrary design in the events of the novel applies to the Stevens-Linda story as well. Stevens seems to be able to tell that Linda will have one glorious love affair and lose her lover and grieve forever after. This she does when she loses her sculptor husband, who dies fighting against Franco in the Spanish Civil War.

New generations have now come, and old ones have gone. Besides Linda Snopes and her advent, Chick Mallison is now a fully participating adult; Hub Hampton, Jr., is now the sheriff, and Mink's daughter is now madame of a whorehouse in Memphis. Faulkner earlier re-used and re-examined his characters from novel to novel without concern for the passage of time, for the saga principle in the record of a family. Quentin Compson, for instance, is revealed at the same point of time in both *The Sound and the Fury* and *Absalom, Absalom!*, as is Mr. Compson, his father. Nancy Mannigoe seems to have been revived almost unchanged in *Requiem for a Nun*, and Gavin Stevens is no older apparently in his appearances in *Light in August, Knights Gambit, Requiem for a Nun*, and *Intruder in the Dust*. This technical difference suggests a shift from timeless human exploration, analysis of states of mind, to a time-conscious survey which seems much more sociological.

Why has Faulkner chosen to create this atmosphere of fatality, and why has he moved forward the time of his action so obviously in *The Mansion?* One of the answers to the latter question is that Faulkner has come to the end of a trilogy and wishes to make it quite clear that it is a trilogy and that this is the end. But the answer to both the above questions lies more accurately in Faulkner's desire to demonstrate that no action is without consequences, that the world that men seek to create is the one that they do create and that this one is usually bad. *The Mansion* is not really a Snopes novel; that is, it is not really about the Snopeses and their misguided ways. Flem is not really striving any more—he has reached the goal of his ambition. He is now, ironically enough, trusted and respected, so much so that he may be caretaker of Jefferson's money and representative of its "good name." Mink has now completed all his suffering. Linda is now free of her father,

168

and Gavin and Ratliff no longer are engaged in quite the same desperate struggle against Snopes' values.

The Mansion is the story of aftermath, the summary and tying up of consequences. *The Hamlet* and *The Town* recorded the history of Snopes progression, of victory and defeat and success. Now we are shown the costs of that career. Flem has really gained nothing when he has gained everything, and the suffering that he has caused is considerable. Mink has found no peace and is still forced back into the role of killer after thirty-eight years. Gavin and Ratliff end only with a sense of loss, a knowledge of human fraility and incompetence, even though that knowledge is full of pathos. The mansion is returned to its owners, who no longer really want it. Appearances still make more impression that reality. The people of Jefferson are no purer or stronger or happier than they ever were, nor have they learned one whit from their encounter with Snopesism. Rather the contrary is true, and they have turned what should have been an enmity into an amity. Flem has become one of them, fully adopted into the heart of the community. The dreadful pointlessness of three generations of suffering, from Ab Snopes to Linda, from the Compsons and De Spains of Jefferson's beginnings to the Jason Compson of the present, is what Faulkner wants very desperately to convey to us. Faulkner has in mind a set of alternatives even while he tries valiantly to keep them out of this novel.

Although the style of the novel is narrative rather than discursive, Faulkner still cannot refrain from the sententious statement, usually coming from Gavin Stevens, but occasionally coming from his nephew Charles, who is, I am afraid, beginning to sound more and more like his uncle. It is from these occasional aphorisms and sermons that we can glimpse the same sentiments that Faulkner has all along suggested as holding the promise of a richer, more meaningful way of life than the one that is revealed in the crass materialism and dreadful respectability of Frenchman's Bend and Jefferson. Now even Ratliff has taken to moralizing and rhetorical usage. Faulkner used to permit himself the privilege of using elaborate diction and syntax in order to convey his character's state of mind. That was entirely appropriate. Now the characters themselves use that language once reserved for Faulkner, and the result is the destruction of convincing character. Unless Ratliff has been around Gavin Stevens so much that he has picked up his manner of thought and speech, it seems entirely inappropriate that he should use a phrase like "last desperate instinctive hereditary expedient."[5] Ratliff also tends towards the moral sentiment, becoming, like Gavin, another of Faulkner's mouthpieces:

> They was church folks. I mean, they went to church a heap of Sundays, and Wednesday night prayer meeting too, unless something else come up. Because church was as good a place as any to finish up one week and start another especially as there wasn't no particular other place to go on Sunday morning.[6]

Surely Gavin is William Faulkner when he says, "Just to hate evil is not enough. You—somebody—has got to do something about it."[7] Even Montgomery Ward Snopes has become self-conscious and downright masterful in his use of words, almost a sympathetic character:

> So the one true bitch we had was not a bitch at all but a saint and martyr, the one technically true pristine immaculate unchallengeable son of a bitch we ever produced wasn't even a Snopes.[8]

Faulkner, then, in this novel is still waging an interior civil

[5] *The Mansion*, 121.
[6] *Ibid.*, 121.
[7] *Ibid.*, 307.
[8] *Ibid.*, 87.

war between his imaginative artistic inclinations and his desire to cater to his own moral awareness, a desire made more
intense by an awareness of his international reputation and
the almost captive audience this position gives him. He is
like a preacher, high up in the pulpit, wanting desperately to
go down and mingle with the crowd, but knowing that they
are looking up and waiting for the sermon which he must give.

There is, in *The Mansion*, no mistaking the humanistic
themes which underlie this pathetic account of the human
struggle. Charles Mallison says, "So what you need is to learn
how to trust in God without depending on Him."[9] and earns
his uncle's approval. This is the nearest thing to a key statement on Faulkner's position, in or out of his work. What specific religious code or dogma or label it indicates I do not
know, but it is exactly what Faulkner has always tried to illustrate and now has stepped forth boldly and ill-advisedly to
say. One of the stories told in *The Mansion* concerns the mirac-
ulous appearance of Christ in the guise of a soldier who appears to a marine sergeant during the war. The sergeant is in
a desperate combat situation, and "He" comes to his assistance. What does the new "undisguised" Faulkner Christ say?:

> We're already full up with folks that know they can but dont,
> since because they already know they can, they dont have to
> do it. *What we want are folks that believe they cant, and then
> do it. The other kind dont need us and we dont need them. I'll
> say more: we dont even want them in the outfit.*[10] (Italics are
> mine.)

The Mansion is a failure for several reasons. The two main-
plot lines bear little real relationship to each other. The Gavin
Stevens and Linda Snopes story is meant to provide a contra-
puntal effect to the Mink story and to indicate to the reader

[9] *Ibid.*, 321.   [10] *Ibid.*, 280.

171

an alternative to the loveless way of life elsewhere presented. The same technique was used quite effectively in *Light in August*, but there it was successful for two reasons. Each story was told with power and beauty, and there were enough characters who convincingly crossed the story lines to make the whole blend complexly and richly together. This is not true of *The Mansion*. Gavin Stevens is meant presumably to provide a contrast to the barren pointlessness of Snopes existence by his rich meaningful movement towards a kind of aged wisdom. But Faulkner never reaches the real Stevens as he reached Benbow or Quentin Compson. Rather this Stevens is a highly self-conscious observer of a situation in which he is supposed to be submerged. You cannot, however, be King Lear and the fool at the same time. When Ratliff of *The Hamlet* becomes involved and drawn in towards the center of the social storm, he ceases to be the detached observer of the early part of the novel, and he ceases to be a character of humor. The wry, sardonic, village sage is replaced by a more frenzied participant, chased from his neighboring security in the boardinghouse by the chaos and fury of the spotted horses, a symbol of Snopesism. The skill of this portrayal was not to reappear in Faulkner's work.

Another failure of *The Mansion* is that the characterization is very weak. Now, as I have tried to show, not just one but several characters have become commentators à la Gavin Stevens—fewer people than ever are convincing participants in the action. And every now and then an observation or commentary is included that has little or no bearing whatever on the action and is merely an obvious Faulkner view inexcusably incorporated:

> . . . Lawyer said, the best of music, from the mathematical inevitability of Mozart through the godlike passion of Beethoven and Bach to the combination bawdy-house street-carnival uproar

172

that Wagner made—that come straight to the modern virile northern Aryan's heart without bothering his mind-a-tall.[11]

But in spite of all these weaknesses there is in *The Mansion* a sufficient amount of splendid writing and storytelling to convince us that it is not Faulkner's talent that has diminished so much as his good judgment. The story of Mink is almost as good as anything else Faulkner has written, and the novel ends with a passage of transcendent beauty that recalls the best descriptive writing of Faulkner's greatest years. The last great paragraph of Faulkner fiction that we have is thus a significant indication of the talent that the author could call upon when he yielded to his masterful imagination.

But he could risk it, he even felt like giving it a fair active chance just to show him, prove what it could do if it wanted to try. And in fact, as soon as he thought that, it seemed to him he could feel the Mink Snopes that had had to spend so much of his life just having unnecessary bother and trouble, beginning to creep, seep, flow easy as sleeping; he could almost watch it, following all the little grass blades and tiny roots, the little holes the worms made, down and down into the ground already full of the folks that had the trouble but were free now, so that it was just the ground and the dirt that had to bother and worry and anguish with the passions and hopes and skeers, the justice and the injustice and the griefs, leaving the folks themselves easy now, all mixed and jumbled up comfortable and easy so wouldn't nobody even know or even care who was which any more, himself among them, equal to any, good as any, brave as any, being inextricable from, anonymous with all of them: the beautiful, the splendid, the proud and the brave, right on up to the very top itself among the shining phantoms and dreams which are the milestones of the long human recording—Helen and the bishops, the kings and the unhomed angels, the scornful and graceless seraphim.[12]

[11] *Ibid.*, 132.   [12] *Ibid.*, 435–36.

CHAPTER IX

The Reivers

"A gentleman accepts the responsibility"

The *Reivers* is Faulkner's only thoroughly comic novel. The nearest thing to it in some ways is *Intruder in the Dust*. *Intruder* also has as its central character a small white boy whose mentor is a wise Negro of mixed descent, and it, too, has a kind of project undertaken jointly by conscience-driven friends, both black and white. But where *Intruder* has for its plot and its obvious motivation the solution of a murder mystery, and the freeing of a wrongly accused Negro, *The Reivers* is on the surface a "much ado about nothing" story. The nothing turns out to be everything, or rather the confusion of the complicated and seemingly pointless action is a means for decisions and discoveries of the most significant kind. Again and again Faulkner's narrator emphasizes and insists on this very disparity between the trivial nature of their activity and the agonies that were involved for its participants.

The importance of this technique can be discussed later, but the point that I wish to make now is that Faulkner never loses sight of his over-all comic intention. One is reminded in this particular case of Fielding's *Tom Jones* and *Joseph Andrews* or even, perhaps, of *Don Quixote*, the greatest picaresque hero of them all. What Fielding and Cervantes and Faulkner have in common is the ability to view with irony and compassion the struggles of man as a contest between a pigmy combatant and a giant circumstance. In such works the world becomes a vast stage on which the actors thrash around in time and space seeming to go nowhere, ending up back home on the doorstep. Their real journey has taken place, of course, outside of space and time, in the mind or soul. The comic writer must be aware of the incongruity of physical action and spiritual discovery. Most of all he must have a vision of the entire race engaged in a variety of frenzied activity with a kind of savage persistence and endurance. The comic vision requires, more than anything else, perspective.

Faulkner, in *The Reivers* as elsewhere, conveys most powerfully his sense of astonishment at the irresistible resilience of the human spirit. He shows us again in this last novel his sense of wonder at human endurance and hope, his constantly renewed surprise at the spiritual strength of man who, like the Titans, seems to bounce back with renewed vigor at each apparent overthrow. From the godlike perspective of the writer, the sheer oppressive weight of circumstances seems overwhelming, and he writes in order to convey his astonishment at his own creations. Faulkner demonstrates conclusively in *The Reivers* (though Faulkner criticism will probably be reluctant, as always, to come to terms with this) that his world view is neither an optimism nor a pessimism, but a humanism, a comprehensive acceptance of the human condition as a meaningful phenomenon, perhaps even a general delight at the variety and interest of life itself and a recognition that nothing but impossible and overwhelming difficulty could merit the engagement of untiring man. Only the greatest writers have had this kind of imagination, and when it has worked as it does in *The Reivers*, it should, perhaps, be called the comic imagination. The over-all outlook does not vary, but the techniques and expression and mood vary in Faulkner as they do in Shakespeare. In *The Reivers* (as opposed say to *The Sound and the Fury*), Faulkner maintains his distance. The characters are not analyzed; there is no attempt to examine their psychological make-up. We take them as we find them—good, bad, odd, even. One is reminded of Chaucer, especially the Chaucer of the "General Prologue," who takes a delight in the whole panorama of the human miscellany and seems to welcome even his most unpleasant characters because they are necessary to complete the color and amusement and significance of a world of "sondry folk."

But more than any other writer, Faulkner in his comic vein reminds one of Dickens. The comparisons are many and perhaps obvious, in spite of the absence of any thorough critical treatment of the similarities. Dickens, more than any other writer, consistently employs the comic imagination. The entire company of Dickens' characters are odd, bizzare. There is no "normal" for Dickens; everyone is special and peculiar. There is only the "furious motion of being alive," the wonder and mystery of life being lived. The artist as artist is surely at his best, his most complete, when he is sufficiently and strangely removed to see the ironies of this antlike struggle and the all-important consequences for the individual.

The structure of *The Reivers* reminds me very much of *David Copperfield*. The grandfather of the Faulkner novel is, like David, a spokesman for the artist, telling a story about the past, in which he was involved, but over which he now casts an appraising glance, a glance of understanding gained through perspective. The narrator sees his past peopled with strange and significant creatures, each of whom played an important role in making the speaker whatever he is in the present. The whole in each case adds up to a story of human encounter with, and survival of, evil, and the education of a sensitive protagonist in the matter of values. This sense of comprehensiveness, the feeling of size, of an ordeal survived and absorbed as valuable experience, is felt only by the reader of the greatest fiction. *As I Lay Dying* is of this kind and of all the works since *A Fable, The Reivers* is nearest to it.

Faulkner's last novel, subtitled *A Reminiscence,* is about a journey, set in the past, told in the present by a narrator who looks back and tells the story perhaps in order to assess and recapture its real significance. It maintains with almost absolute consistency the child's point of view. The agonies of conscience, the size and importance of all one's acts and decisions, and the intense concern for the codes and rules and one's own integrity are all brilliantly conveyed by the old man trying, like Faulkner, to tell how it was, what the experience was all about, and how frustrating and impossible it is to tell it, trying to wrench and turn and force the recalcitrant language into explaining what one felt and what it means. Grandfather Priest tells how when he was a boy the automobile came to Jefferson and how his grandfather at the time was forced to own one. He was forced, one might notice, by the kind of consideration that Faulkner everywhere deplores, a neighbor contest that makes people buy things they do not want and contributes to the general dishonesty on which society is constructed. In any case, the purchase of the unwanted automobile is in many ways a kind of good-bye to the past; evil begins casually enough.

When all the white overseers, the family authority, are gone on a trip to a funeral, Boon Hogganbeck and Lucius Priest take the car and proceed with it to Memphis, accompanied by Ned McCaslin, the negro retainer who stows away and reveals himself en route. The plot proceeds to be a rapid multiplication of unlikely circumstances, a kind of zany farce in which Ned swaps the stolen automobile for a stolen race horse and a race in which to enter it. The story of Reba's Memphis brothel provides its own forms of amusement and insight, and then the locale shifts to Parsham, a village which is to be the scene of the race. The idea is to win back the automobile and thus have both it and a horse too, which will be something to show for the trip and enable them to return home and face the discordant music.

All the trouble and difficulty to which they are forced, merely to return home, when in fact they need never have left, leads Lucius to wonder at the mystery of this self-created confusion. So many people are dragged in, so many quiet lives disturbed, and so much conniving and suffering and physical hardship occurs that the whole affair would seem to escape rational comprehension.

The Reivers is not an allegory, but it is a metaphor, or at least it is centered on one. The answer to the "why" of all this activity is the same existential answer as to the why of living itself. Substantially the aim of the characters is to end where they began. There is no real movement, no change, no real getting anywhere, just as for Faulkner there was, I believe, no comforting, easy supernatural answer. There is only the process itself, the activity and its difficulties which provide the protagonists the opportunity to be what Faulkner in this novel calls gentlemen. The only meaning is in the becoming, in the doing, and there is no end to it. The actors must become different for having played their parts, and for them the whole episode will be a kind of toning-up in the business of living. It is as though man were a fighter training in the actual continuous match, in the combat itself, becoming ever better prepared to fight the next bout in a program that has no ending. Frequently Lucius has to remind himself that this is so.

> . . . if we could get the automobile back for no more than just telling Bobo to go get it and be quick about it, what were we doing here? what had we gone to all this trouble and anxiety for? camouflaging and masquerading Lightning at midnight

through the Memphis tenderloin to get him to the depot; ruthlessly using a combination of uxoriousness and nepotism to disrupt a whole boxcar from the railroad system to get him to Parsham; not to mention the rest of it: having to cope with Butch, Minnie's tooth, invading and outraging Uncle Parsham's home, and sleeplessness and (yes) homesickness and (me again) not even a change of underclothes; all that striving and struggling and finagling to run a horse race with a horse which was not ours, to recover an automobile we had never had any business with in the first place, when all we had to do to get the automobile was to send one of the family colored boys to fetch it. You see what I mean? If the successful outcome of the race this afternoon wasn't really the pivot; if Lightning and I were not the last desperate barrier between Boon and Ned and Grandfather's anger, even if not his police; if without winning the race or even having to run it, Ned and Boon could go back to Jefferson (which was the only home Ned knew, and the only milieu in which Boon could have survived) as if nothing had happened, and take up again as though they had never been away, then all of us were engaged in a make-believe not too different from a boy's game of cops and robbers.[1]

At the end of all this, things will not appear to be different, and the quiet processes of Jefferson will absorb the delinquents as a tree eventually grows over the nail driven into it. But somewhere something will have changed—the nail is there, and it does not go away.

True to his persistent outlook, Faulkner in *The Reivers* is not content to illustrate this metaphysic in a purely existential way. He points clearly to human, social benefits and improvements and, like the humanist he is, ends this comedy with a traditional, idyllic image of birth and promise. The new generation, born of the reformed prostitute, will be better in itself and will also find a better world around it as a result of the

[1] *The Reivers: A Reminiscence* (New York, 1962), 229–30.

events of the past. No matter how minutely, Lucius has changed his world, as the new baby's name and, indeed, very presence signifies. It would not exist if Corrie had not turned housewife, and she would not have been redeemed if Lucius had not stolen the automobile and gone to Memphis and encountered the evil of the brothel and defended the honor of a prostitute. Lucius believes and illustrates, on behalf of his creator, that even a prostitute has honor and dignity and pride and that her very humanity should be her defense. What Otis, her nephew, did that so outraged Lucius in relating the story was to spy on her promiscuity and make a peep show of it. This particular brand of economic ingenuity seems to have represented for Faulkner a special kind of low in human behavior and is brutally illustrated in *The Hamlet* also. The reason is probably that it suggests a cold, inhuman detachment that the unwitting performers do not themselves have and that Faulkner's own humanity and taste found particularly offensive. To sin with passion because one is weak or lonely or bored or frustrated is one thing. That is human. To cold-bloodedly exploit that weakness is another. That is inhuman. Lucius' code is Faulkner's, and his fighting for it is the turning point of Corrie's life. She is even able to return to her own name, Everbie Corinthia, and able to be herself now that she has found somebody who is willing to fight and obtain for her her human privileges, somebody with no thought or possibility of personal advantage.

The story of *The Reivers* is, of course, the story of Lucius, which is why he tells it. As an account of what happens to a child it is, like *Intruder*, a parable of initiation and the discovery of evil. The novel does indeed remind one of nothing so much as the myth of the Fall. It is, in fact, a comic prose version of the loss of Paradise and the consequences thereof. Even more than in *Intruder* one is forced to recall Huck Finn and his journey of discovery, also told in the first person, also made in the company of a paternal Negro, and also ending in a sense where it began. Like the *Adventures of Huckleberry Finn*, the novel seems to be a metaphor on several levels, with racial and local themes as well as universal ones. The Jefferson of the novel's beginning seems, indeed, to be a kind of paradise: a place of order and security, of rigid moral codes, and of complicated but well understood systems of honor. The whole atmosphere of this section has a deliberately contrived fairy-tale quality. The mishaps and the violence are modulated as though heard from far away over autumn fields. The material is "legendary" (Faulkner used the shooting incident in "The Bear"), and there is an insular quality to the livery stable and the square; even the district names of McCaslin and Hampton and Beauchamp and Bookwright are comfortable, and their owners are comfortably doing the things that people bearing such names must do—being sheriff, running banks, and making whisky. This atmosphere is even able to absorb and overcome the automobile itself, though it does come from outside, and it takes on the coach pattern of genteel rides and Saturday outings, in spite of the need to screen the ladies against Grandfather's tobacco-spitting.

The automobile, however, like the apple in Eden, represents the temptation to greater knowledge. Here is the means to the outside world. With speed comes an end to local isolation. With the automobile comes the road, and roads go somewhere. True to their human nature and following the pattern of Adam himself, Boon and Ned and Lucius cannot resist the temptation to greater knowledge. They take the car and set out for Memphis. On the way they must pass a place called "Hell Creek Bottom," not pass it but go through it because, as Boon says, "Hell Creek Bottom ain't got no around." Boon makes so much of it and the problems of crossing it because Faulkner wishes to convey the significance of this obstacle in the novel's structure. It represents a kind of gateway to the underworld, and the keeper of this gate, the ferryman of Yoknapatawpha's own Styx, is a mule driver who farms mud so that he can rent mules. There is no bypassing him. He names his own terms, and the automobile helplessly waits on the efficiency of mules. This probably means nothing more than that Faulkner prefers mules to cars, but the entire passage is so elaborated, brilliantly comic and ironic though it is, that it conveys by design a sense of enormous distance traveled, a feeling of really having left the old world behind.

Memphis always seems to represent a symbolic underworld in Faulkner's fiction. It is in Memphis that evil is fully encountered: unattached, unmodified evil. Evil in Jefferson or Frenchman's Bend is evil with a setting, a background, an opposition. Evil in Memphis is the thing itself, and one's education depends on a visit there. The cold, nonhuman quality of the city once suggested to Faulkner the figure of Popeye in *Sanctuary*; now it suggests Otis, a similar, runtlike fifteen-year-old from Arkansas, wise in the ways of corruption and, like Popeye or Flem Snopes, undisturbed by the human qualities of compassion or love or even appetite. His disinterested materialism is an aspect of, or an adjunct to, a kind of impotence, more clearly indicated in Snopes and Popeye, but felt strongly enough in the portrait of Otis. When, therefore, Lucius fights Otis, he is fighting on behalf of, not only Corrie herself, but the very humanity and frailty she represents, fighting against the principal of the antihuman. Lucius has carried with him into the fallen world the best of his impulses and his precedents, and with them he is of value there. The symbolic stake in this struggle is Corrie herself. Lucius restores her to herself, changes her way of life, gives her new self-respect and dignity, and makes her happy in fact. The comic vein makes it necessary that Otis be easily defeated. Faulkner cannot aesthetically afford the kind of struggle in which Flem Snopes engages in *The Hamlet*. Otis defeats himself, really, by his own avarice and cowardice. The theft of the tooth is an interesting parable. For Otis the gold tooth of Minnie represents whatever value it has to a buyer with money. To Minnie it represents more even than the years of saving that were required to buy it—it is a symbol of her own independence, a visible testament to her persistence and courage.

> She had beautiful teeth anyhow, like small richly alabaster matched and evenly serrated headstones against the rich chocolate of her face when she smiled or spoke. But she had more. The middle right-hand upper one was gold; in her dark face it reigned like a queen among the white dazzle of the others, seeming actually to glow, gleam as with a slow inner fire or lambence of more than gold, until that single tooth appeared even bigger than both of Miss Reba's yellowish diamonds put together.[2]

Otis, the pure materialist, cannot of course know how much the tooth means, because he is simply unequipped to realize that there can be that much feeling about anything. He is doomed, therefore, to lose because Minnie, and Reba also, who realizes what it means, will not be defeated: "So when he heard the train whistle, he run, huh? Where do you figger he is? Because I'm going to have Minnie's tooth back."[3] One does not envy poor Otis!

The real story might well have ended there, and Lucius might have gone home with the same amount of education as he has by the end of the novel. But Faulkner extends this basic situation in order that the reader as well as the participants will have undergone a sense of trial, of extended tension. The pressures of living and the ability to survive them and use

2 *Ibid.*, 100.
3 *Ibid.*, 202.

them must be conveyed by extended repetition and elaboration so that by the end the reader, like Lucius, has a remarkable feeling of having undergone a major experience. This extension enables Faulkner to introduce the real function of Ned and the reason for his presence on the trip. Because when it comes to coping with apparently hopeless circumstances and to meeting suffering with fortitude, it takes someone like the Negro, who not only has suffered all his life because of an accident of birth, but has behind him a rich heritage of suffering upon which to call.

Ned is the subsequent overseer and guide. It is he who obtains the horse and turns what was meant to be a harmless jaunt into a major excursion into life. It is Ned who wins the horse race, who makes Lucius a jockey, who educates Boss, and he must do all this in the face of the Sheriff's lust, the general hostility to strangers, the avarice of Otis, the reluctance of the horse itself, the pressures of time, and the attitude toward his own color.

It would be a pity to distort the comic mode and effect of the novel by a critical analysis. I have tried to suggest that Faulkner very consciously seeks to maintain the comic vein. Nevertheless, this intention cannot obscure the serious themes and attitudes which underlie all else, and the reader cannot help being fully aware of them, as he is in any great comic work. Again and again Faulkner has his characters present the powerful affirmation that has become a kind of trademark of his later writing:

> There are things, circumstances, conditions in the world which should not be there but are, and you cant escape them and indeed, you would not escape them even if you had the choice, since they too are a part of Motion, of participating in life, being alive.[4]

4 *Ibid.*, 155.

The entire design of this novel is meant to be an assertion of the validity of life, of the value of being alive, and of the use and usability of suffering, and happily Faulkner has here avoided yielding to the urgency of this outlook. To a great degree the novel is free from the sententious moralizing of thinly disguised spokesmen that has characterized his later work. It was, I believe, in order to avoid this tendency that Faulkner finally chose the broad comic method. He does not avoid it entirely, however, and the novel is weakened whenever that Stockholm voice is heard, all too clearly. For instance, that voice breaks from the narrative to utter a protest at modern anonymity and hypocrisy, because people once accepted death as a natural part of life and faced it with more courage:

> Not to mention the husbands and uncles and aunts in the twenties and thirties and forties, and the grandparents and childless great-uncles and -aunts who died at home then, in the same rooms and beds they were born in, instead of in cubicled euphemisms with names pertaining to sunset.[5]

The voice comes in early to suggest the social responsibility that everyone must learn:

> . . . the idea (not mine: your great-grandfather's) being that even at eleven a man should already have behind him one year of paying for, assuming responsibility for, the space he occupied, the room he took up, in the world's (Jefferson, Mississippi's, anyway) economy.[6]

And the voice returns at the end to say with a kind of symbolic finality in Faulkner's last novel: "Nothing is ever forgotten. Nothing is ever lost. It's too valuable."[7] We are almost being

[5] *Ibid.*, 44–45.
[6] *Ibid.*, 4.
[7] *Ibid.*, 302.

reminded by the grandfather that we, like Lucius, have been told the entire story to enable us to learn this point. After all, the Lucius of the story is himself a grandfather, retelling the story to a boy who may in turn tell it again. In effect Faulkner creates an echoing backwards and forwards through the generations. We do not know this great-grandfather, we do not know just what has led him to such a deep-rooted conviction. This is a technical weakness in the novel. But the same conviction, or at least an affirmation of the same life principle, occurs at the end of *The Wild Palms*, written twenty-three years earlier:

> Not could. Will. I want to. So it is the old meat after all, no matter how old. Because if memory exists outside of the flesh it wont be memory because it wont know what it remembers so when she became not then half of memory became not and if I become not then all of remembering will cease to be.—Yes, he thought, between grief and nothing I will take grief.[8]

This is the powerful conclusion to a long train of thought which is moving and telling because it comes from a man with whom we have been intimate and whose suffering we have witnessed. We know him well enough to have been involved. Faulkner used to conceive of characters and situations first and their discoveries were their own, rising naturally from their experience and nature. The contrived quality of character and incident and language only becomes a characteristic later on—theme produces a demand for form rather than form implying an integral theme as it once did.

Perhaps the most interesting and even exciting feature of *The Reivers* as an expression of Faulkner's outlook is his final attempt to describe the ideal humanist. Faulkner does here arrive at something close to a definition, and he does so, not by

[8] *The Wild Palms* (New York, 1939), 324.

abstract speculation, but by telling how a man must act. He falls back on the term "gentleman," and it seems as good a term as any.

A gentleman can live through anything. He faces anything. A gentleman accepts the responsibility of his actions and bears the burden of their consequences, even when he did not himself instigate them but only acquiesced to them, didn't say No though he knew he should.[9]

Faulkner's gentleman sounds like Chaucer's knight. Faulkner believed that not only is such a model a possible reality, it is an absolute essential. Man is dependent on his own efforts to be a gentleman both for personal meaning and survival and also for racial purpose and improvement. A gentleman, too, fails, but he does not give up; he suffers, but he still hopes; he makes errors, he sins, but he is never lost. Faulkner sums it all up in a superb metaphor that might stand as a kind of subtitle to the entire body of his work: " 'A gentleman cries too, but he always washes his face.' " And the next sentence is "And this is all."[10]

[9] *The Reivers: A Reminiscence*, 302.
[10] *Ibid.*, 303.

CHAPTER X

Conclusion

A conclusion is doomed by its nature, perhaps, to be a rather dreary reiteration of previous statements. In this case, however, some repetition may be useful, since I am trying to counter a widespread tendency to read Faulkner in one of two ways: either to see him as a nihilist or as a Christian optimist. Of these two views the former is by far the more common. The advantages for critics who thus read him are that they can simplify and separate the elements of his work and that they have ready-made labels, for example, pessimist, optimist, nihilist, fatalist, anticapitalist, agrarian, and so on. I also have been forced to lean rather heavily on a term, humanist. But I have tried to suggest that finally the term is only partially satisfactory. What term is there for a humanist who is motivated by faith, for a believer in God who denies churches or dogma or orthodoxy, for a reformer who denies utopias? These are aspects of William Faulkner's outlook. Faulkner believes both in free will and individual responsibility and social determinism; he believes in the possibility of social and physical improvement and the eternal sameness of individual struggle and fulfillment; he believes in the necessity of faith, and he rejects the absolutes of rigid theology. Faulkner emerges as a religious man without a religion and a humanist without a rational dialectic. The reason for the difficulty in presenting Faulkner's convictions is that ultimately they defy analysis. Faulkner was well aware that he was no philosopher. He was a poet, if the term may be applied to any literary artist of great sensibility, and as such he responded with his whole being to specific situations. Faulkner did not decide that automobiles were a destructive force in human affairs or an economic factor or a social, graceless irritation; he simply disliked them. After he disliked them, he decided that they were antihuman. Faulkner did not in the first place speculate about avarice, materialism, rapacity, hypocrisy, cowardice, or urbanization—he saw them in concrete instances and felt hostile. Faulkner did not decide through any ratiocinative process that the Southern Negro's brand of religious faith was necessary for us all—he merely saw it. He saw that it made suffering not only endurable but meaningful, and he admired it. If Faulkner has written any great work, it is precisely because in that work he refused to compromise his convictions or submerge them in any kind of system. To propose any system for him is then to grossly distort his views. To represent Faulkner honestly, one must confine oneself to terms like view, attitude, and conviction rather than system or idea.

What finally demands our attention in Faulkner's whole production is the consistency with which he has presented these attitudes. Whether it be an attempt to systematize or rationalize these views, as in his later work, or dramatize and mythologize them, as in his early work, they are nevertheless always there and always basically the same. It is my belief that close textual reading will reveal, as I have tried to show, that this outlook is positive, that Faulkner accepts the paradoxes which he incorporates and that he believes in a meaningful universe, a universe subject to a design which is nonetheless real for not being readily apprehensible or easily demonstrable. I have tried, then, to present as fully as I can the attitude of Faulkner toward life as he saw it and to show how this outlook is the motivating force in his later work. Faulkner said on many occasions that he was a frustrated poet. If he had been able, I believe, he would have said what Wordsworth said in "Tintern Abbey,"

> *And I have felt*
> *A presence that disturbs me with the joy*
> *Of elevated thoughts; a sense sublime*
> *Of something far more deeply interfused,*
> *Whose dwelling is the light of setting suns,*
> *And the round ocean and the living air,*
> *And the blue sky, and in the mind of man:*
> *A motion and a spirit, that impels*
> *All thinking things, all objects of all thought,*
> *And rolls through all things.* (Lines 95–104)

I believe that these lines represent almost exactly the spirit, if not the letter, of Faulkner's thinking.

A great many critics have understood Faulkner totally differently. There has been a widespread tendency to mistake the part for the whole, to seize upon the great number of negative images and mistake them for Faulkner's statements when they are in reality his whipping boys. It derives, I think, from a refusal on the critics' part to grant the writer the great intelligence and control which he must surely have had, and while this is a fate not peculiar to Faulkner, few writers have suffered more misrepresentation because of it. The most common reading of this kind might be called Faulkner's "cosmic pessimism," and it is best represented in the valuable book by Campbell and Foster.[1] They devote an entire chapter to this thesis, and it contains such characteristic conclusions that it is worthy of some detailed attention here.

Campbell and Foster first suggest that of possible views of the world Faulkner's "belongs to the pessimistic variety."[2]

[1] Harry Modean Campbell and Ruel E. Foster, *William Faulkner, a Critical Appraisal* (Norman, 1951).

[2] *Ibid.,* 114.

That is to say that he portrays man "as the tragic victim of a chaotic (if not malignant) universe just as likely to harm as to aid him during the course of his short life and at all events providing nothing more than eternal annihilation at its end."[3] I think these terms misleading. Where Faulkner has "victims," he is careful to point to specific man-made evils as the cause, but for the moment let us accept the terms. The authors then go on to recognize that there are in Faulkner's work certain characters who seem to rise above the general gloom, and these they call "morally good" characters. However, the morally good characters likewise suffer a hopeless fate:

> The fact that some of Faulkner's morally good characters escape actual tragedy may to some extent relieve the cosmic pessimism, but even for these there is nothing ultimately more hopeful than self-respect (Isaac McCaslin, Byron Bunch) or a rather imperceptive complacency (Lena Grove, all of the Negroes except perhaps Dilsey).[4]

Now all this raises the question of Faulkner's role as the writer of tragedy. To suggest that the hero in literature be given some obvious external reward in order that his creator avoid the title "pessimist" is to undermine the affirmation of all great tragic literature. Self-respect, or perhaps meaning through suffering, is always the reward of the tragic hero. In fact, what makes him a hero is his ability to learn from his suffering. Tragedy is not pessimism. Sophocles is not a pessimist and certainly not a believer in cosmic chaos simply because he shows Oedipus suffering and outcast. In fact, the reverse is true: Oedipus suffers because the world is subject to order. The suffering of the tragic hero elevates the audience as well as arouses its compassion because it is meaningful, and

[3] *Ibid.*, 114.
[4] *Ibid.*, 115.

meaning is all that the great writer demands or believes in or urges. In a way, to remark the absence of what Campbell and Foster call "cosmic compensation" is to imply that in order to be positive, writing must be comic; for only in comic writing is there "cosmic compensation." Actually we need not grant the absence of such compensation. I suppose "cosmic" here means mysterious or rationally inexplicable: the fulfillment of Lena's quest, the safety of the tall convict in *The Old Man*, the escape of the little boy from under the hooves of the spotted horses, the survival of Dilsey, the safety of Isaac before the bear; surely these are a few of many instances of what could be called, among other things, "cosmic compensation." But in a way the term "cosmic" is itself misleading in this context. Man is surely a part of the cosmos, and it is quite possible to see God working through man and nature as, say, Emerson and Thoreau do. Must rewards be external to man to signify "cosmic optimism"? Surely self-respect is no slight prize to extract from life.

Campbell and Foster quite accurately recognize the "paradoxical tension between determinism and individual responsibility," a tension that is certainly part of Faulkner's work, and then they observe that "since some of the indisputably innocent suffer quite as much as those who might possibly be considered to possess a modern variant of the 'tragic flaw,' the cosmic situation still remains gloomy."[5] But Faulkner has gone to elaborate lengths to show that the innocent are victims of men, not of the cosmos, and his interest in the victim is to a large extent an interest in the specific causes of the suffering. Quentin Compson, who is one of the examples, is a specific illustration of his father's nihilism, but Mr. Compson must not be mistaken for Faulkner himself. In order that he should not be so mistaken, Faulkner has provided the section on

5 *Ibid.*, 115–16.

Dilsey; her vision is conveniently ignored by a surprising number of critics. Quentin is, in fact, neither entirely innocent nor in any sense heroic. His suffering is meaningless for him, he has no "tragic flaw," but is flawed throughout; and while he arouses our pity, he does not, and is not meant to, evoke our admiration. Time and again Faulkner has illustrated his belief in the possibility and necessity for man to rise above his origins and circumstances. Characters like Quentin are designed to show the results of a failure to do so.

This insistence on free will is, ironically enough, precisely the burden of a passage which Campbell and Foster cite for entirely different reasons:

> I know what you will say. That having Himself created them He could have known no more of hope than He could have pride and grief but He didn't hope He just waited because He had made them: not just because He had set them alive and in motion but because He had already worried with them so long: worried with them so long because He had seen how in individual cases they were capable of anything any height or depth remembered in mazed incomprehension out of heaven where hell was created too and so He must admit them or else admit His equal somewhere and so be no longer God and therefore must accept responsibility for what He Himself had done in order to live with Himself in His lonely and paramount heaven.[6]

Ike is saying that God, in order to retain his self-respect (which in his case involves the unenviable position, lonely and paramount) must give man free will or admit the equal power of the devil, in which case man would be a pawn in a divine chess game. Ike is anxious to establish this point in preparation for his justification of relinquishment.

Mistaking Faulkner for his characters can lead to widespread misunderstanding; one might, after all, choose one

[6] *Ibid.*, 116.

character as well as another. One must, I think, make some distinction between the strong, forthright, and sententious statements of characters who are merely spokesmen, voices clearly intended to speak for the author, and those statements that may reflect back on the speaker when he is a well realized character, fully integrated into a novel's theme and action. Gavin Stevens, Cousin McCaslin, and Grandfather Priest are clearly of the former kind, as is the late Ratliff. Almost none of the early characters appear in this way. In the early work a whole novel speaks for Faulkner; in the later work characters speak for him. The critical failure to make this distinction has led to much confusion. The following is an example of this tendency.

> For the characters, and perhaps for the author, there appears to be some slight degree of relief in attempting to fix the ultimate responsibility for tragedy: there is always a villain, though, even within the same indictment, he may shift from man to God, depending on who becomes the victim; as when Miss Rosa Coldfield, speaking of Sutpen's downfall, says that he "created in his own image the cold Cerberus of his private hell," but she considered herself, ruined by Sutpen, as cosmically the victim of "that justice whose Moloch's palate-paunch makes no distinction between gristle bone and tender flesh . . . that sickness somewhere at the prime foundation of this factual scheme."[7]

But Rosa's present condition is the result of her own ambition; loneliness and greed and her present incarceration is a voluntary act signifying the ludicrous outrage of her Southern, feminine pride. It is the same kind of reaction that Caroline Compson would have manifested. Here again it is necessary to be aware of the great care and precision with which Faulkner presents the details of character and situation and to re-

[7] *Ibid.*, 117.

member that *Absalom, Absalom!* is entirely constructed of fragments of point of view.

The failure to give this artistry its due is again noticeable in the reading of Faulkner's metaphors.

> Thus, as Mr. Compson says of the early career of Sutpen, "while he was still playing the scene to the audience, behind him Fate, destiny, retribution, irony—the stage manager, call him what you will—was already striking the set and dragging on the synthetic and spurious shadows and shapes of the next one." Both Sutpen and the stage manager, it seems, are performing rather poorly, and in view of his vastly superior power and responsibility for the whole performance, the stage manager looks worse than the actor.[8]

There is no reason to think that Faulkner chose this metaphor without an awareness of all its implications, and no reason, therefore, why we should not take them into account. A stage manager does not choose sets, he merely drags them on and places them. Nor does a stage manager choose or write the play. The stage manager (a term indicating Compson's cynicism, not Faulkner's) is the kind of God represented much later in *A Fable*, who merely accedes to the wishes of man; man, especially in the South, wrote this particular play, which is now being aped or acted out by Sutpen with the stage manager waiting in the background for his cues. Mr. Compson refuses to admit the existence of God, and so avoids the term. But at the same time he would like to deny human responsibility and free will. As Quentin finds out, his father's views are of no help to him. A similar example of textual misunderstanding occurs in connection with a quotation from *Mosquitoes*. While the general observations of Campbell and Foster about the quality of this work are undoubtedly justi-

[8] *Ibid.,* 117–18.

fied, their misinterpretation of specific metaphors must be noted because it suggests how many critics come to their conclusions about Faulkner's views.

> When David and Mrs. Maurier's niece leave the ship for a walk on the land, they move among "huge and silent trees," which "might have been the first of living things, too recently born to know either fear or astonishment, dragging their sluggish umbilical cords from out the old miasmic womb of a nothingness latent and dreadful." The Passage is obviously intended to suggest that the petty, futile lives of these trivial characters is symbolic of a similar dreadful futility in the whole universe.[9]

But the passage is not obviously so intended. The couple are not going for a walk, they are running away. These characters are not meant to be trivial, they are rebels against a trivial society, the microcosm of the ship, and are driven by their love to the wilderness, where mosquitoes drive them back again. Love is therefore unable to survive in this hostile world. The whole situation is contrived and unsatisfactory, but that general artistic weakness has nothing to do with the meaning of the metaphor in question. The trees are grand primeval things of the wilderness that have struggled against nothingness to produce themselves by an agonized birth. This is a picture of southern Louisiana swampland, a version of the painful birth of the world out of chaos. There is nothing futile or trivial about the emergence of life out of nothing.

Another and different example of common misreading of Faulkner is the emphatic insistence on one passage as opposed to another, or on a part as opposed to the whole. It is a disregard of context as in the following reference to *Soldiers' Pay*.

[9] *Ibid.*, 120.

In *Soldiers' Pay*, for example, as the rector and Gilligan walk through the countryside after the funeral of Mahon, the rector's son, they hear the singing in the Negro church. The simple faith of the Negroes even to the religious rector seems ironical after the horrible tragedy in the maimed life and the death of his son. "Then," says the author, "the singing died, fading away along the mooned land inevitable with tomorrow and sweat, with sex and death and damnation; and they turned townward under the moon, feeling dust in their shoes."[10]

How this faith comes to appear ironical is not at all clear, and the spirit of the passage is entirely obscure until one reads the whole last paragraph of the novel.

Feed Thy Sheep, O Jesus. The voices rose full and soft. There was no organ; no organ was needed as above the harmonic passion of bass and baritone soared a clear soprano of women's voices like a flight of gold and heavenly birds. They stood together in the dust, the rector in his shapeless black, and Gilligan in his new hard serge, listening, seeing the shabby church become beautiful with mellow longing, passionate and sad. Then the singing died, fading away along the mooned land inevitable with to-morrow and sweat, with sex and death and damnation; and they turned townward under the moon, feeling dust in their shoes.[11]

Surely there is an enormous, compassionate acceptance of the human lot signified even here in this early and slight novel. It is not what is outside that matters, it is what is in there with the Negroes of the church. What the Negroes have, Gilligan and the rector do not have, and this "minister of God" is not inside but outside the church. The rector and Gilligan are not Faulkner.

Finally, it is perhaps necessary to point out the inevitable confusion that results from an attempt to reconcile the positive

[10] *Ibid.*, 119.
[11] *Mosquitoes* (New York, 1927), 169.

aspects of Faulkner's myth with an insistence on an interpretation of "cosmic pessimism."

> ... this idea of endurance is nothing new for Faulkner. The Lenas, Dilseys, and Miss Jenny DuPres have been "prevailing" all along in his work; there are simply more of them in his last three books. But even in these last (and in some respects rather sentimental) books, the morally good (and therefore to some extent happy) characters are represented as being a very small group—indeed, a scanty remnant— in a predominantly evil world, one in which the good accomplished by this remnant receives no support from the universe or any hypothetical power outside the universe. In these works, too, cosmic pessimism is still the main element in Faulkner's philosophical attitude.[12]

This statement seems to suggest that Faulkner's "philosophical attitude" is one of "cosmic pessimism" because (a) the number of "morally good" characters is small and (b) they receive "no support from the universe or any hypothetical power outside the universe." But what have these two conditions to do with each other? Would a greater number of "morally good" characters eliminate the need for supernatural support? Or would their significance increase with an increase in their number? Surely divine intervention would undermine the significance of their moral goodness. Moreover, what reason is there to suspect that Lena and Dilsey are ironic victims of an empty delusion in their belief? Their faith is presented quite seriously, and it seems to work for them. When Milton justifies the ways of God to man, he does not suggest that Adam understand His mysterious ways. His belief is enough. Dilsey, Sam Fathers, Lena, Nancy, the Corporal, Charles Mallison, Byron Bunch, Rosa Millard, Lucius Priest, Gavin Stevens, and Ratliff cannot be written off as a scanty remnant. The truth of the matter is that terms like pessimism and opti-

12 Campbell and Foster, *William Faulkner*, 138–39.

mism and "ultimately more hopeful" and "morally good" have little relationship to Faulkner's work. The great tragic or comic themes have to do with discovery and meaning. Suffering must be productive, man must rise above his apparent limitations, and responsibility and free will produce a human dilemma without which there is nothing. Life is good, not because it always works out well, or because it is progressive (it does not, and it is not), but because it is all there is, all man knows, and without it there is nothing. Faulkner wholeheartedly accepted it:

> Think of all that has happened here, on this earth. All the blood hot and strong for living, pleasuring, that has soaked back into it. For grieving and suffering too, of course, but still getting something out of it for all that, getting a lot out of it, because after all you dont have to continue to bear what you believe is suffering; you can always choose to stop that, put an end to that. And even suffering and grieving is better than nothing; there is only one thing worse than not being alive, and that's shame. But you cant be alive forever, and you always wear out life long before you have exhausted the possibilities of living. And all that must be somewhere; all that could not have been invented and created just to be thrown away. And the earth is shallow; there is not a great deal of it before you come to the rock. And the earth dont want to just keep things, hoard them; it wants to use them again. Look at the seed, the acorns, at what happens even to carrion when you try to bury it: it refuses too, seethes and struggles too until it reaches light and air again, hunting the sun still.[13]

"Cosmic pessimism" might be applied to Hardy or Hemingway, but it simply misrepresents the spirit of Faulkner's writing. Destructive criticism for its own sake is at best a waste of time, but the refutation I have been attempting is,

[13] *The Big Woods*, 137.

I hope, necessary and constructive. I have, of course, done no more here than reassert the contentions of earlier chapters, but it is important to point out again and again the vastness of Faulkner's vision which amounts to a resounding, compassionate "yes" to life and man. Faulkner's convictions became more assertive, but they are not new, and perhaps they were always a threat to his artistry, so that *The Sound and the Fury* might be a greater or more perfect novel without the Dilsey section. Even in spite of its beauty, it seems a little like a postscript to a vision, a vision where everything, even evil, is fascinating and beautiful. But the moralist who is glimpsed in the story of Dilsey is seen all too clearly later on, and the more insistent the moralist, the weaker the artist. The moralist tried to make intellectually apprehensible what the artist had imaginatively conceived and presented as metaphor. The artist wants the metaphor to make its way in the world as well as it can; the moralist does not trust art to get very far or help man very much. The war between these two was a real and continuous one in Faulkner's case, and neither side won any final victory. The important thing is that moralist and artist both were part of William Faulkner, and no matter which held temporary ascendancy, the writing that emerged was always affirmative; his whole production amounts to the kind of all-encompassing affirmation that one associates with only the greatest writers before him, a vision of life that incorporates and transcends the moral diversity of its details. It is my hope that a better understanding of this affirmation, seen as it is most clearly in the later works of Faulkner, may lead the reader to a richer appreciation of the entire phenomenal unity which his writings compose. There is no bequest in our time more worthy of our attention and appreciation.

Index

William Faulkner: A Study in Humanism, from Metaphor to Discourse has been set in eleven-point Caledonia, a distinguished type face designed exclusively for the Linotype by W. A. Dwiggins, the eminent American graphic artist.

This book is printed on paper bearing the watermark of the University of Oklahoma Press and is designed for an effective life of at least three hundred years.

UNIVERSITY OF OKLAHOMA PRESS
Norman